# Meditation
## A Practical Guide to a Spiritual Discipline
### ⌒ Quiet Times for Forty Days ⌒

Thomas McCormick
Sharon Fish

*InterVarsity Press*
*Downers Grove*
*Illinois 60515*

© 1983 by Inter-Varsity Christian Fellowship of the United States of America

All rights reserved. No part of this book may be reproduced in any form without written permission from InterVarsity Press, Downers Grove, Illinois.

InterVarsity Press is the book-publishing division of Inter-Varsity Christian Fellowship, a student movement active on campus at hundreds of universities, colleges and schools of nursing. For information about local and regional activities, write IVCF, 233 Langdon St., Madison, WI 53703.

Distributed in Canada through InterVarsity Press, 860 Denison St., Unit 3, Markham, Ontario L3R 4H1, Canada.

ISBN 0-87784-844-0

Printed in the United States of America

| 17 | 16 | 15 | 14 | 13 | 12 | 11 | 10 | 9 | 8 | 7 | 6 | 5 | 4 | 3 | 2 | 1 |
|----|----|----|----|----|----|----|----|---|---|---|---|---|---|---|---|---|
| 95 | 94 | 93 | 92 | 91 | 90 | 89 | 88 | 87 | | 86 | 85 | 84 | 83 | | | |

# Acknowledgments

*I wish to acknowledge with gratitude the early support given to this project by the Finaghy Evangelical Presbyterian Church in Belfast, Ireland, and Norman and Angela Reid in Dublin. My friends and teachers at Westminster Theological Seminary also deserve a word of thanks, as do those pastors and elders who have shepherded my soul. My wife, Penny, has contributed insight, literary savvy and hours of typing as well as regular encouragement for which I am very grateful. Above all, our gracious and merciful God is to be praised for his sovereign and steadfast love revealed in Jesus and for his living Word, the Bible.*

Tom McCormick

# Introduction

Should Christians meditate? If so, how? These questions have arisen over the past few years largely in response to the influx of various Eastern (and quasi-Eastern) religions into the Western world. In other generations the answers to these questions would have been taken for granted. Now, however, our society has become so infiltrated with forms of meditation not based on biblical principles that Christians need to reinvestigate this time-honored tradition.

The studies in this book are meant to assist you in searching out what the Scriptures say about meditation. They are not only, however, *about* meditation; they are intended themselves *to be* meditations. They are meditations on meditation. Because we are eager that the Holy Spirit be your teacher, some of the questions are open-ended. As Martin

Luther has said, "It often happens that I lose myself in such rich thoughts [literally, "that my thoughts go for a walk"] in one petition of the Lord's Prayer and then I let all other six petitions go. When such rich good thoughts come, one should let the other prayers go and give room to these thoughts, listen to them in silence and by no means suppress them. For here the Holy Spirit himself is preaching and one word of His sermon is better than thousands of our own prayers. Therefore I have often learned more in one prayer than I could have obtained from much reading and thinking."

As you work through these studies, keep in mind that God has guaranteed that there will be results in your life! He has promised us "every spiritual blessing" (Eph 1:3) and all that is needed for "life and godliness" (2 Pet 1:3). And the God who gave us his own Son has also given us all things with him (Rom 8:32). Simply put, God's way of life, as given to us in the Bible (which includes meditation), is sufficient—it is all we need. The promises given specifically to those who meditate as God has directed are indeed rich and abundant. Included in those promises are success and prosperity in all we do (Josh 1:8; Ps 1:3), wisdom, understanding and the knowledge of God (Ps 49; 119:97-100; Prov 3:8), guidance and protection (Ps 19:11; Prov 6:20-22), even life itself (Ps 19: 7, 14; Prov 3:22). What more could be asked? The promises of God, however, are received by faith, and often in weakness (2 Cor 12:9). Thus, on the one hand, we can confidently expect all we need, with God himself as our teacher (Jn 16:13). On the other hand, we must be prepared to humble ourselves if we are to experience the reality and fulfillment of these promises of God (Jas 4:5-10). Surely this is as true for our life of meditation as for our Christian life in general.

The studies in this book are designed to help you obtain these spiritual blessings. Each study begins with two quotations—the first from Scripture and the second from another source. These quotations are given to help open your thoughts on the particular topic of each study. While we do not necessarily agree with every detail of each nonscriptural quotation, we do think that they provide a helpful catalyst for thought. Following the quotations are some suggested hymns. Feel free to sing or read them at the beginning or the end of your study (or both!). Or use other hymns of your choice. Singing, too, is a form of meditation. At the end of each study there are suggestions for further study. These could be used later the same day, or as a separate daily devotion.

You may decide to follow our order of studies, or you may want to skip around. If you are a "dabbler," though, keep in mind that some of the later studies build on the early ones. If you skip ahead, you may need to return to an earlier study to understand the full import of the later one. Whatever order you choose, keep a journal or a note pad handy to record the progress of your thoughts and feelings. Often in meditation you will have valuable thoughts which you will not want to forget. Writing them down fixes them for future reference and frees your mind for new considerations. Writing helps us to clarify just what it is we do think, forcing us to be precise, and even stimulates discovery as we enter into a dialog with ourselves. Writing also gives us a record which we can refer to in the future, sharing with others or just remembering and meditating on what we have thought and what God has taught us. We encourage you to write in response to and during your meditations; however, do not become enslaved to such a suggestion, since our thoughts are sometimes more hindered than helped by the demand to write. Some questions in this study guide may stimulate thoughts which you will want to keep. Write them down; follow the tangents which emerge. Other questions you may want to ponder in silence and stillness.

The studies are divided into four topics. The first part, "The Life of Meditation," deals with some basics about what meditation is and how it can be applied to real-life situations. The second part, "Objects of Meditation," takes a deeper look at the things on which we meditate. "Images of Meditation" deals with the figurative language used to present meditation in Scripture. This part involves a different way of thinking, a more literary way than some are perhaps used to. But the studies, even if somewhat more difficult, are just as practical as the others in this book. The final section covers some special principles of meditation, aspects which will round out your practice of meditation as well as your understanding.

Because meditation is a varied and complex process, the style of these studies also varies. Meditating on creation is not the same as meditating on God's law; nor is meditating on a specific object like meditating on a certain image.

In spite of the variety, however, you will find that certain key Scripture passages recur throughout the book. This reflects another aspect of meditation—focus on a single object from various perspectives. By incorporating this basic structure of meditation—variation within repetition—into the book as a whole, we hope to enrich your practice and understanding of meditation.

Closely related to this basic structure of meditation is a fundamental characteristic of Hebrew poetry whose beauty and usefulness will be recognized throughout this book. This characteristic is most often called *parallelism* and has been described as thought-rhythm, one thought being matched, echoed or somehow completed by another. Though the variety of types of parallelism is seemingly endless, three types are noted here, each of which occurs in the passages to be studied. The first type is *synonymous parallelism*, in which the second line "simply reinforces the first, so that its content is enriched and the total effect becomes spacious and impressive,"* as in Psalm 103:10:

He does not deal with us according to our sins,
nor requite us according to our iniquities.

The second type is *climactic parallelism*, in which the second line mounts higher than the first, adding to or enlarging upon the first line. This is illustrated by Psalm 145:18:

The LORD is near to all who call upon him,
to all who call upon him in truth.

The third type of special interest to our studies is *antithetical parallelism*. This type is quite common in Proverbs (chapters 10—31), but is also found in Psalms. As its name suggests the two lines give antithetical or opposite views on the issue in question. Psalm 37:21 illustrates this nicely:

The wicked borrows, and cannot pay back,
but the righteous is generous and gives.

When the question of parallelism arises, a consideration of these three types can be helpful for a first approximation. Remember, though, the variety of types is much broader than these three. Learning these patterns and using them in your meditations will reward you with much new information and joy.

A word of caution. Meditation takes time—and so do these studies! If you are unwilling to spend at least thirty to forty-five minutes on each study, then your meditation (and your relationship with God) will be minimally enriched. Be aware, however, of the possibility of spending *too much* time. Each study contains the seed material for many hours of intense meditation and study. Follow the advice of the Puritan who said: "Do not overdo in point of violence or length; but carry on the work sincerely according to the ability of your minds and bodies; lest going beyond your strength, you craze your brains, and decompose your minds, and disable yourselves, to do anything at all. Though we cannot estimatively love God too much, yet it is possible to think of Him with too much passion, or too long at once, because it may be more than the spirits and brain can bear.... You little know how lamentable and distressed a case you will be in, or how great an advantage the tempter hath, if once he do but tire you by overdoing."

These studies are merely beginnings. Even "Further Study" just scratches the surface of the wealth of biblical material on meditation and for meditation. The rest is up to you.

"The purpose of a book of meditations is to teach you how to think and not to do your thinking for you," said Thomas Merton. A lifetime of mining the unsearchable riches of God's wisdom is yours.

* *Derek Kidner*, Psalms 1—72 *(Downers Grove, Ill.: InterVarsity Press, 1973), p. 3.*

# I
# The Life
# of Meditation

When should we meditate? Where? Why? On what? Are there certain situations or problems we face that could be resolved if we spent more time with the Lord, thinking about his past involvement in our lives, his presence, his promises, his commands?

These introductory studies will help you focus on a few basic principles of Christian meditation and on a variety of circumstances that prompted people to meditate. As you study and reflect on the passages, be aware of key principles of meditation. You can apply these to your own thoughts and actions when facing similar situations today or in the coming weeks.

Think also about the people involved. What were they like? What qualities characterized their lives? How do these character traits relate to meditation? What do you have to do to build these same qualities into your life? How can your meditations become more pleasing to God, and your life more fulfilling and fruitful?

Some of the principles touched on in these introductory studies will be more fully developed in other sections. Our initial aim is to give you a general overview of the purpose and process of meditation. Through selected psalms, proverbs and other Old and New Testament passages, you will observe people who knew their God because they cared enough to spend time with him, pondering his majesty and works, treasuring his words, yielding to his lordship over all of life.

# 1
# The Meditator

*Blessed is the man*
*who walks not in the counsel of the wicked,*
*nor stands in the way of sinners,*
*nor sits in the seat of scoffers;*
*but his delight is in the law of the LORD,*
*and on his law he meditates day and night.*
PSALM 1:1-2

*As [meditation] is every man's work, so it is every day's*
*work. . . . David saith that his meditation was at*
*work all the day long: "It is my meditation all the day." . . .*
*Yea, in Psalm 1 he takes in the night too: "He delighteth*
*in the law of the LORD, and therein doth*
*he meditate day and night."*
WILLIAM BRIDGE

Suggested Hymns
*Take My Life, and Let It Be*
*Take Thou Our Minds, Dear Lord*

**1.** Each verse of Psalm 1 tells you something about the meditator, portraying his character through positive statements (v. 2), negative contrasts (vv. 1, 4-6) and figurative language (v. 3). To begin your study, read slowly through the psalm. Let your mind dwell on each verse, noting the meditator's character, activity and lifestyle.

**2.** Reflect on the things the psalmist does not do (v. 1). Reformulate these expressions in your own words, considering their application to your life in today's society.

In contrast to these things, what *does* the psalmist do (v. 2)? The type of contrast found here is a particular form of Hebrew poetry known as antithetical parallelism. The word *but* serves as a pivot point between the positive and negative aspects of the contrast. Keep this form in mind as you trace the theme of meditation throughout the Scriptures.

**3.** From these verses and parallel passages we learn that meditation is not simply a passive, quiet state or discipline but an active process encompassing all activities of life. Turn the negative statements about the blessed man in verse 1 into positive statements, and you will discover more of what meditation involves.

**4.** What is the specific object of the psalmist's meditation (v. 2)? When does he meditate? Where? The answer to the last question, while not explicit, is implied in verses 1-3.

**5.** Reflect on the attitude of the one who meditates on God and the things of God, specifically the law. What does the phrase *delight in* convey to you? What would be some synonyms for *delight*?

Make a list of specific things you delight in, such as ice cream, a special friendship, sunsets, newborn babies, puppies. What prompts you to delight in each thing? How is your delight different in each case?

**6.** Delight is a common and precious human experience. Meditating is a form of delight. Whatever we delight in we think about and seek after. Gradually our lives become more and more centered around our hearts' desires.

How would you describe your own relationship to the Scriptures? What can you do to bring your relationship with God's Word more into conformity with that of the meditator in Psalm 1?

## Further Study

**1.** The activities of verse 1 not only characterize what Christian meditators do not do; they also indicate what would hinder Christian meditation. If you have trouble meditating, consider whether you are "walking," "standing" or "sitting" in ways that will not be blessed.

**2.** Consider developing the positive counterparts to the activities described in verse 1 by studying what Scripture says about these activities. For a start consider the following:

*walking,* Galatians 5:16-25, Ephesians 5:1-2, 15-20; *standing,* Ephesians 6:10-20, especially verses 11 and 14; *sitting,* Ephesians 2:4-7.

**3.** Compare Psalm 92 with Psalm 1. What does the psalmist do "day and night" in Psalm 92:1-2? How are the wicked contrasted with the righteous (vv. 5-9)? How is the tree image used in relation to the righteous (vv. 12-15)? In each case note the similarities and differences between these two psalms.

# 2
# The Meditation Process
## (Part I)

*I will meditate on thy precepts,*
*and fix my eyes on thy ways.*
PSALM 119:15

*If Psalm 119 is read as though it were lyrical or epic poetry,*
*the reader is sure to be disappointed. For every letter*
*of the Hebrew alphabet, the psalmist has written eight verses*
*beginning with the letter. The letters change, but the*
*subject remains the same! With seemingly monotonous in-*
*sistence the psalmist keeps praising the law of the Lord.*
*The key to understanding the psalm is to enter into the kind of*
*meditation that produced it. The pattern of the psalm is*
*similar to the method that has been called "Lotus meditation"*
*in the East. The meditator centers his mind on one subject;*
*he reflects on many relationships and aspects of the subject,*
*but keeps coming back to the central thought. The pat-*
*tern of his thought keeps looping back to the center like the*
*petals of a lotus flower. Speed reading is guaranteed to*
*destroy the force of the psalm by reducing its deliberate reflec-*
*tion to a blur of synonyms. But the meditating reader*
*can follow the psalmist's path afresh and be directed and in-*
*formed in his own reflections on the Word of God.*
*EDMUND P. CLOWNEY*

Suggested Hymns
*Spirit of God, Descend upon My Heart*
*Like a River Glorious*

**1.** Psalm 119 directs our thoughts to a specific object of meditation we will look at in greater detail in part three. In addition to teaching us how to relate to this object, the psalm
teaches us much about the process of meditation. The psalm

itself is a meditation. Read the first three stanzas (vv. 1-24) several times to get a feel for the thought patterns of the psalm. Then read them aloud. Read them silently, slowly, prayerfully. Pause to reflect after each eight verses.

Notice the similarities of the opening verses of Psalm 119 with Psalm 1. What other similarities do you notice between the two psalms?

**2.** Psalm 119 is an *acrostic*. It is divided into twenty-two parts, one for each letter of the Hebrew alphabet. Each part has eight verses, all of which begin with the same Hebrew letter.

The word *meditate* or *meditation* is used eight times in the psalm, for the first time in verse 15. Read through the second stanza (vv. 9-16). What does *each* verse contribute to your understanding of the psalmist/meditator? his motives and attitude? his primary desire? his activities? How do you compare to this person?

**3.** According to verses 9-16, what are some results or anticipated benefits for those who meditate?

**Further Study**

**1.** Eight different words are used for the object of meditation in this psalm. What are they?

**2.** Only one of the 176 verses does not contain one of these eight words. Can you find which verse that is?

# 3
# The Meditation
# Process
## (Part II)

*I revere thy commandments, which I love,*
*and I will meditate on thy statutes.*
PSALM 119:48

*Meditation is that exercise of the mind by which it*
*recalls a known truth, as some kind of creatures do their*
*food, to be ruminated upon, till all vicious parts be extracted.*
*BISHOP HOWE*

Suggested Hymns
*Breathe on Me, Breath of God*
*O for a Closer Walk with God*

**1.** Read Psalm 119:41-48. Consider all the ways the meditator relates to the Word of God in this stanza. What do these verses tell you about the process and purpose of meditation?

Notice how prayer is interwoven throughout these verses. Is the entire psalm a meditative (or contemplative) prayer addressed to God? Explain. Keep this question in mind as you investigate other portions of this psalm.

**2.** Focus on verses 15-16. Both the activity of the psalmist and the object of his considerations are expressed in different ways. These are not four different activities or four different objects but four ways of expressing different facets of the same activity and object. Reflect on these unique nuances and what contributions each makes to your understanding of the practice of meditation.

Throughout the psalm the variations of expression will continue to enrich your understanding of meditation. This pattern of repetition and variation will be developed more fully as a basic principle of meditation in part four.

**3.** Continue your study of this psalm, focusing on verses 17-24.

☐ What words or phrases are similar in meaning to *meditate?* Keep in mind the principles of parallelism.

☐ What implicit or explicit contrasts are there to *meditate* or *meditation?* Recall the principle of antithetical parallelism.

☐ What seems to be the situation of the meditator? What problems or needs prompt his meditations?

☐ What does the psalmist meditate on? Note the variety of expressions he uses for the same object.

☐ When does the psalmist meditate? Where?

☐ What are the results or effects of meditation in the life of the meditator?

☐ What is the meditator's attitude toward and response to the object of his meditations?

**Further Study**

**1.** Each stanza of Psalm 119 can be a fruitful study and meditation for you. Focusing on one stanza a day, use the questions in question 3 to help you progress through the psalm.

# 4
# The Way of Wisdom

*My son, keep your father's commandment,*
*and forsake not your mother's teaching.*
*Bind them upon your heart always;*
*tie them about your neck.*
*When you walk, they will lead you;*
*when you lie down, they will watch over you;*
*and when you awake, they will talk with you.*
*For the commandment is a lamp and the teaching a light,*
*and the reproofs of discipline are the way of life.*
PROVERBS 6:20-23

*Meditation is a soul-fattening duty; it is a grace-strengthening duty, it is a duty-crowning duty. Gerson calls meditation the nurse of prayer; Jerome calls it his paradise; Basil calls it the treasury where all the graces are locked up; Theophylact calls it the very gate and portal by which we enter into glory; and Aristotle, though a heathen, placeth felicity in the contemplation of the mind. You may read much and hear much, yet without meditation you will never be excellent, you will never be eminent Christians.*
THOMAS BROOKS

Suggested Hymns
*Be Thou My Vision*
*Go Labor On: Spend, and Be Spent*

**1.** Psalm 119:9-16, Psalm 1 and Proverbs 1—3 (esp. 1:1-6; 2:1-15) all focus on a similar topic. What general theme underlies all three passages?
**2.** Not every occasion of meditation in the Scripture is signaled by the word *meditate*. There are, however, many words and phrases which are similar in meaning. We have already seen some examples in Psalm 119:9-16: "laid up thy word in my heart," "delight in," "fix my eyes on," "not forget." Now

note the words or phrases similar to the concept of meditation in Proverbs 1:8-9; 2:1-5; 3:1-2, 21-24. In each instance note what the son is directed to meditate on and what is promised for faithful obedience to these directives.

**3.** Proverbs 1—3, like Psalms 1 and 119:9-16, focuses on the lifestyle of the godly person. Such a life is governed by biblical wisdom. Each verse or unit of thought in Proverbs is a condensation of such wisdom, a nugget of great worth. These brief yet pithy sayings can be excellent aids to meditation. While the attention and focus is confined to a specific subject or object, application can be multifaceted. Choose one or two of the proverbs in chapters 1—3 for your daily meditation. Dwell on each thought, reaching deep for its meaning. Memorize the verse. Learn the wisdom of it. Apply it to your life.

**Further Study**
**1.** Read Proverbs 4—9. What themes do you see continued here that were introduced in Proverbs 1—3? What more do you learn about meditation?

**2.** You may want to read a chapter a day in Proverbs in addition to your other study or meditation. This way the entire book can be read in a month. Such reading should not, however, take the place of in-depth meditation on a verse or phrase.

**3.** Compare the New Testament concept of wisdom with what you have learned in this study of Proverbs. 1 Corinthians 1:18-31 would be a good place to start. Consider also 2 Timothy 3:15-17; James 1:5-8; 3:13-18.

# 5
# Facing Life's Perplexities

*But when I thought how to understand this,*
*it seemed to me a wearisome task,*
*until I went into the sanctuary of God.*
PSALM 73:16-17

*Devotional meditation transforms our perceptions of*
*the world, the events of our lives, our own existence.*
*EDMUND P. CLOWNEY*

Suggested Hymns
*Be Still, My Soul*
*Jesus, I Am Resting, Resting*

**1.** Read Psalm 49. What situation prompted the psalmist to meditate? What riddle or problem confronted him (vv. 5-20)?
**2.** It is often assumed that true meditation transcends the rather mundane aspects of life and should not, or perhaps even cannot, be uttered or expressed in any comprehensible manner. Thus meditation is assumed to be a strictly private affair as we commune with God alone in our hearts. In scriptural language the heart does frequently refer to the innermost aspect of a person, the depths and roots of one's being and the origin of thought and action. But the heart is also used as a designation for the whole person, and the meditations of one's heart (or inner person) can often be shared with others. As we gain understanding of the world and the events of our lives through meditation, our mouths should utter

wisdom to help others deal with the perplexities of life. Christian meditation is not beyond thought or beyond language. Out of the fullness of our hearts our mouths should speak wisdom born of our meditations on God and the things of God, and our lives should bear fruit (see Mt 12:34).

Note all the words and phrases in Psalm 49:1-4 that refer to audible expression. To whom is the psalmist addressing himself?

**3.** What aids to meditation does the psalmist employ in solving the riddle (v. 4)? What is there about each that could be a valuable asset to the process of meditation? (Part four, no. 37 develops this point.)

**4.** Verses 5-20 give us the context of the psalmist's meditations on one of the perplexities of life. What conclusions does he come to as a result of his meditations on the riddle?

**5.** What does this psalm say to you about your own priorities, desires and plans? How have you considered them in light of the psalmist's conclusions? In what ways do you share the hope of the psalmist (v. 5)?

**6.** Spend a few minutes thinking about questions you would like to have answered. What riddles in life do you want solved? What questions would you like answered? Some of your questions may be related to fundamental issues of how the universe works, such as why God allows suffering and evil in the world. More personally, you may be perplexed about why God allowed a certain event to take place in your life or why he has withheld something you feel you need. These can be opportunities for meditation as you seek God's perspective of the situation through his Word and through communion with him.

If music has not been part of your devotional experience, this might be a good time to explore this as another aid to meditation. Many of the great hymns of the church are condensations of complex theological truths that can give you insights into many of life's perplexities. Include songs from Scripture in your hymn singing.

**Further Study**

**1.** Consider various New Testament meditations on similar themes found in Psalm 49, for example: 1 Corinthians 15; James 5; 1 Timothy 6:17-19; Matthew 6:19-21. What different perspectives and contributions do these passages offer on the themes of Psalm 49? on the process of meditation?

# 6
# Facing Responsibility

*Have I not commanded you? Be strong and of good courage; be not frightened, neither be dismayed; for the LORD your God is with you wherever you go.*
*JOSHUA 1:9*

*When I tread the verge of Jordan,*
*Bid my anxious fears subside;*
*Bear me through the swelling current,*
*Land me safe on Canaan's side:*
*Songs of praises, songs of praises*
*I will ever give to thee.*
*WILLIAM WILLIAMS*

Suggested Hymns
*Guide Me, O Thou Great Jehovah*
*He Leadeth Me*
*If Thou but Suffer God to Guide Thee*

**1.** Read Joshua 1:1-9. What situation was Joshua facing? What might have been some of his thoughts and feelings after the death of Moses? (See Deut 34:1-12 for background reading.)
**2.** What did God command Joshua to do? What promises did God give to Joshua personally and to the people of Israel? (See also Deut 31:7-8.)
**3.** What do verses 6, 7 and 9 imply about possible reactions Joshua might have had to his responsibilities?

What commands and promises does God reinforce for Joshua in verse 9? How could meditating on (i.e., remembering and pondering) the various promises of God help Joshua be obedient to what God expected him to do?
**4.** What specific object of meditation is mentioned in verses

7-8? What do these verses say about this object of meditation in the following areas?
☐ The time for meditation.
☐ The purpose of meditation.
☐ The outcome of meditation.
☐ The motivation for meditation.
**5.** Read Joshua 1:10-18. How does Joshua respond to what God has said? What does Joshua command the people to do in verse 13? Note their response to Joshua.
**6.** What situation are you facing that bears similarities to Joshua's? How have you been feeling about it? Be honest! Has God given you any commands or promises? Consider the specific commands and promises God gave to Joshua that you listed for question 2. Personalize them in the light of your own situation and spend time meditating on them.

**Further Study**
**1.** The New Testament develops these same ideas, often in quite similar language. Consider: Ephesians 6:10-20; 2 Corinthians 12:9-10. Further promises and counsel are given to those facing responsibility in such passages as James 1:5-8; Philippians 4:19; Hebrews 13:5-6.
**2.** Consider the comparison between Joshua and Jesus given in Hebrews 4.

# 7
# Facing Anxiety

*Look at the birds of the air...*
*MATTHEW 6:26*

*Said the robin to the sparrow*
*"I should really like to know*
*Why these anxious human beings*
*Rush around and worry so?"*

*Said the sparrow to the robin*
*"Friend I think it's plain to see*
*That they have no heavenly Father*
*Such as cares for you and me."*
*A GERMAN HYMN*

Suggested Hymns
*Peace, Perfect Peace*
*When Morning Gilds the Sky*

**1.** Read Matthew 6:25-34 and Luke 12:22-34. How would you characterize the disciples? What do you learn about their attitudes and primary concerns? Note Jesus' appraisal of them.

Now spend a few minutes reflecting on your own situation. What specific things caused you anxiety this past week? Why? Were these anxieties in any way related to material possessions or basic needs for safety and security? How did you deal with your anxiety? Was the way you dealt with your anxiety helpful or harmful to yourself? to others?

**2.** What does Jesus tell his disciples not to do? Why?

**3.** What words or phrases in these passages are the same as or similar to *meditate*? What specific objects of nature does Jesus urge his disciples to meditate on? Why these?

What conclusions should our meditations lead us to about

God's care and concern for us? about our attitudes and actions in relation to our possessions? (Note: In Palestine, grass was burned as fuel.)

**4.** What does Jesus urge his disciples to seek? What does this seeking involve?

Reflect on Luke 12:32-34. What treasure(s) do you find your own heart (thoughts, meditations) set on? Do your attitudes and actions reflect this?

**5.** Now think about any situation you are facing today or will be in the coming week that may cause you to be anxious. How are you going to deal with this situation in light of this passage? How could spending time this week meditating on God's care and concern for you in the past prevent undue anxiety in the present and the future? Meditate on God's meeting your most basic needs, and ask God to strengthen your faith and show you how to truly seek his kingdom this week in thought, word and deed.

**Further Study**

**1.** Jesus faced times of great trial and temptation. No doubt he also faced temptations to anxiety (Heb 4:15). Consider how Jesus faced one of his most anxious times by comparing Matthew 26:36-46, Mark 14:32-42 and Luke 22:39-46.

**2.** Paul too faced intense anxiety. Consider Paul's descriptions in 2 Corinthians 11:23-29 (cf. Acts 16:16-40), and his counsel on dealing with anxiety in Philippians 3:7-11, 20-21; 4:4-9; 2 Corinthians 12:7-10. Also consider 1 Peter 5:7.

# 8
# Facing Life's Uncertainties

*Behold, I am the handmaid of the Lord; let it be to me*
*according to your word.*
LUKE 1:38

---

*Meditation that does not face squarely grief, fear, doubt,*
*and anger cannot lay hold of God's blessing.*
EDMUND P. CLOWNEY

---

Suggested Hymns
*A Mighty Fortress Is Our God*
*My Faith Looks Up to Thee*
*O God, Our Help in Ages Past*

---

**1.** Read Genesis 24:62-67. What situation might have prompted Isaac to meditate? What might have been some of the thoughts on his mind? (Read Gen 23:1-2, 19; 24:1-4 for background clues.)

**2.** Where was Isaac when he meditated? When was he meditating? What might be the significance of both the time and place to the process of meditation?

**3.** Read Luke 1:26-38. What situation was Mary facing? Note her emotional and intellectual response to the angel's message. What phrase in verse 29 is similar to *meditate*? How would you characterize Mary's attitude of heart revealed in verse 38?

The Word of God, which we will consider in greater detail as a primary object of meditation, is no ordinary word but, like the words of the angel to Mary, is alive and active, searching our hearts and calling forth obedience (cf. Heb 4:12).

**4.** Reflect on Luke 1:39-56. Note Elizabeth's appraisal of Mary in verse 45. Has the Lord spoken to you recently through his Word? Compare your response to Mary's.

**5.** Mary draws heavily on the Old Testament to express the thoughts of her heart (for example, 1 Sam 2:1-10; Gen 17:7). What does this tell you about Mary and her relationship to the Word? to meditation?

**6.** Have you faced a sorrowful or uncertain situation like Isaac's recently? Are you fearful about the future? Reflect for a moment on any difficult situation which may confront you. Do you believe that God will provide for you? How can you use this situation to open yourself to God's guidance? What role might meditation play in this process?

We are not told the precise content of either Isaac's meditations or Mary's "ponderings." We do get a clue about Mary, however, from her outburst of praise to God. As you ponder your own situation, spend adequate time meditating on the things that will issue in a song of praise in your life.

**Further Study**
**1.** Reflect on Luke 2:19, 51 for further insight into Mary's life of meditation.

# II
# Objects
# of
# Meditation

*"Every man,"* wrote John Fort Newton, *"has a train of thoughts on which he rides alone. The dignity and nobility of his life, as well as his happiness, depends upon the direction in which the train is going, the baggage it carries and the scenery through which it travels."*

In Philippians Paul exhorts the Christians to direct their thoughts along a track that leads to maturity (Phil 3:12-16). What should be the content of our thoughts? Paul doesn't say specifically, but he does give us clues as to the characteristics of the objects we should be thinking or meditating about. *"Whatever is true, whatever is honorable, whatever is just, whatever is pure, whatever is lovely, whatever is gracious, if there is any excellence, if there is anything worthy of praise, think about these things"* (Phil 4:8).

Although there are similarities between Christian and other types of meditation, the distinctives of Christian meditation are especially highlighted by the focus of our attention. The studies in this section consider the objects of meditation which are given in Scripture. These objects have similarities, yet it is also important to note their differences since these reveal variety and freedom *within a biblical view of meditation. Keep alert, then, to the unique contribution of each object as it enriches and broadens the scope of meditation.*

*There is abundant matter for our meditation. . . . Out of these we may choose sometimes one thing, sometimes another to be the particular objects of our thoughts. To undertake more than one at a time will deprive us of the benefit of all. Too much food will destroy rather than increase the natural heat: a little wood may help that fire to burn, which a great quantity would smother.  [George Swinnock]*

# 9
# The Works of God in Creation: Nature
## (Part I)

*O LORD, how manifold are thy works!*
*In wisdom hast thou made them all. . . .*
*May the glory of the LORD endure for ever,*
*may the LORD rejoice in his works. . . .*
*May my meditation be pleasing to him,*
*for I rejoice in the LORD.*
PSALM 104:24, 31, 34

*Earth's crammed with heaven*
*and every common bush aflame with God;*
*but only those who see take off their shoes,*
*the rest sit around it and pluck blackberries.*
ELIZABETH BARRETT BROWNING

Suggested Hymns
*For the Beauty of the Earth*
*God, All Nature Sings Thy Glory*
*This Is My Father's World*

**1.** We are constantly surrounded by objects which are worthy of meditation. These are created by God and reflect his glory to the world. Think about the last time you observed the stars at night, a sunrise, a sunset, fall foliage or some other aspect of creation. Try to recapture your thoughts and feelings of that experience.

**2.** Read Genesis 1:1-25. Spend several minutes thinking about the various things called into being prior to the creation of man. What conclusions do you come to about God's character and abilities by reflecting on what God said and did? on the order in which he did these things? What seems to be God's overall attitude toward and desires for creation?

**3.** Think about our intended relationship to the rest of creation as you meditate on Genesis 1:26-31. Reflect on the purposes of creation from these verses.

**4.** What aspects of creation are mentioned in Psalm 19:1-6? (Note: The firmament was thought of as the vault or arch of the sky, separating the waters in the sky from those on earth. See also Gen 1:6-8, where firmament is a synonym for heaven.) Notice the specific activities involving creation that further define the purposes of nature. How and when do these aspects of creation speak? What do they say?

**5.** Reflect on Psalm 19:5-6. Spend some time thinking about the sun, noticing how the psalmist develops this image through simile. Why is the sun such a fitting object for meditation? How does it show forth the glory of God?

In your experience, how do you see creation fulfilling the commands of Psalm 148? How is the psalmist himself fulfilling God's command given in Genesis 1:28?

**6.** To conclude this study on the works of God in creation, continue to meditate on Psalm 19:1-6, comparing your own responses to God's works of creation with those of the psalmist. Do you find yourself simply taking creation for granted, or do you take time to meditate on the wonderful works which reflect God's glory, wisdom, power, beauty and holiness? Do you ever praise, thank and rejoice in God as a result of reflecting on his creation?

Take time today to meditate on at least one aspect of creation. Let your mental images be a stimulus to personal prayer and praise to the creator and sustainer of the universe. Ask God to make you more aware of him as you pause to reflect today and in the coming weeks on the wonderful works that God himself is rejoicing in.

### Further Study

**1.** Derek Kidner notes with regard to Psalm 104, "The structure of the psalm is modeled fairly closely on that of Genesis 1, taking the stages of creation as starting-points for praise."*

Can you see the correlation between days one to six in Genesis 1: 3-31 and the verses of this psalm?

*Derek Kidner*, Psalms 73—150 *(Downers Grove, Ill.: InterVarsity Press, 1975), p. 368.*

# 10
# The Works of God in Creation: Nature
## (Part II)

*For the wrath of God is revealed from heaven against all
ungodliness and wickedness of men who by their wickedness
suppress the truth. For what can be known about God
is plain to them, because God has shown it to them. Ever since
the creation of the world his invisible nature, namely,
his eternal power and deity, has been clearly perceived in
the things that have been made.*
ROMANS 1:18-20

*I sing the mighty pow'r of God,
That made the mountains rise;
That spread the flowing seas abroad,
And built the lofty skies.
I sing the wisdom that ordained
The sun to rule the day;
The moon shines full at his command,
And all the stars obey.*

*There's not a plant or flow'r below,
But makes Thy glories known:
And clouds arise, and tempests blow,
By order from Thy throne;
While all that borrows life from Thee
Is ever in Thy care.
And ev'rywhere that man can be,
Thou, God, art present there.*
ISAAC WATTS

Suggested Hymns
*All Things Bright and Beautiful
Praise to the Lord, the Almighty*

**1.** The questions for this study continue to focus on the works of God in nature. One motif that underlies all of Scripture is that the created works of God are not meant to be ends, in and of themselves, but means to reveal his glory.

Read slowly through the following passages: Genesis 1:24-31; 3:17-19; 2 Peter 3:10-13; Revelation 21:1. What do they reveal about the past, present and future states of the created works of God?

**2.** Read Romans 1:18-25, reflecting on the following:

☐ What does verse 20 tell you about one purpose of nature? Name some specific things that you could learn, therefore, from meditating on God's creation.

☐ What should our response to nature be (v. 21)? How have people responded (vv. 21-25)? What has been your response?

☐ If we *perceive* who God is but refuse to *receive* this knowledge, what might this say about our meditations? Do Christians who meditate on nature "see" exactly the same as non-Christians? Why or why not? (You may want to reserve judgment on this question until completion of this study or until you have meditated on the passages in study 12 which deal with our fallen and redeemed state.

**3.** Because of Adam's sin, nature as well as humanity is in bondage to sin. Read Romans 8:18-27. What state is creation in now (vv. 20-21)? How might this affect our meditation on nature? What hope is there for nature? for us? for our meditation?

**4.** Nature, though now in bondage and decay, reveals the glory of God and can assist us to proclaim that glory—the truth of who God is. As you conclude your study on the works of God in creation, turn to Psalm 8. Read it slowly and meditatively. Notice the objects of the psalmist's meditations and how this leads him to respond to nature. Spend some time honoring God and giving thanks to him for the revelation of his glory, his eternal power and deity, through the created world around you.

**Further Study**
1. Reflect on Genesis 3:1-7, comparing this passage with Romans 1:18-32, especially verse 25. What has happened to us since the Fall? Spend some time thinking about your own relationship to God. In what way(s) have you exchanged the truth of God for a lie? Confess areas of disobedience. 1 John 1:8—2:2 can assist you.
2. Consider the use of Psalm 8 in Hebrews 2:6-8. In light of the study above, do you think that the portion of Psalm 8 quoted in Hebrews applies only to Christ, or could it apply also to mankind in general? If so, why; if not, why not?
3. Consider the new creation as it is described in the New Testament: 2 Corinthians 5:17; Ephesians 2:8-10; Colossians 1:15-20; 2 Peter 3:11-13; Revelation 21:22.

# 11
# The Works of God in Creation: We Ourselves
## (Part I)

*For thou didst form my inward parts,*
*thou didst knit me together in my mother's womb.*
*I praise thee, for thou art fearful and wonderful.*
*Wonderful are thy works!*
*PSALM 139:13-14*

*Meditate on thy own making, that we may fall in love*
*with our creator.*
*DAVID DICKSON*

Suggested Hymns
*All People That on Earth Do Dwell*
*Praise Ye the Lord, the Almighty*

**1.** As nature proclaims God's handiwork, so do we. We are his workmanship fashioned by God as clay is molded in the hands of a potter, objects of his creativity and love (Eph 2:10; Is 64:8). Created in God's image, we are to reflect his character. As we meditate on ourselves, our self-consciousness should become God-consciousness, turning our hearts to praise, thank, love and rejoice in God our Father who created us, formed us, redeemed us and called us by name. We are his (Is 43:1).

**2.** Psalm 139 is a meditation on oneself. Read slowly through the psalm, noticing all the phrases that include personal pronouns. Note the time span covered by the psalmist's meditations. What aspects of his life does the psalmist think about? What conclusions does he come to as he meditates on each aspect of his own creation and activity? What are his thoughts about God? about others?

Spend some time reflecting on various aspects of your own life that Psalm 139 might prompt you to think about. Direct your thoughts and prayers to God.

**3.** Review Psalm 8. How do the psalmist's meditations on nature lead to incredulity regarding his own creation and existence? As he ponders his own creation, what does he conclude (vv. 5-8)? What is his final response to his meditations? How do you respond to this same knowledge about yourself?

**4.** Psalm 100 is an appropriate psalm to conclude your study. Read it slowly, prayerfully, meditatively, as a psalm of praise and thanksgiving, an acknowledgment of our finiteness yet infinite worth to the God who made us in his own image.

**Further Study**

**1.** Read the account of man's creation in Genesis 1:26-31 and 2:7, 18-24. What do you learn about being created in God's image from these verses?

**2.** Romans 9—11 talks about God's calling certain people to be his. Although this can be a controversial topic, it is rich in material for reflection. Read 9:16-24. What kind of vessel are you? As Christians we are created for beauty and glory (vv. 21 and 23). As you think of ways in which you fail to be this kind of vessel, read the warning of 11:22. What does it mean to continue in God's kindness? How can meditation be a part of that? Indeed there is a complexity involved in God's dealings with us. Paul too found this to be so. End by reading 11:33-36, and join with Paul in praising our wonderful Creator and Redeemer.

# 12
# The Works of God in Creation: We Ourselves
## (Part II)

*For we ourselves were once foolish, disobedient, led astray,*
*slaves to various passions and pleasures, passing our days*
*in malice and envy, hated by men and hating one another.*
*TITUS 3:3*

*God's purpose for man is simply this, that man should be*
*able to say to the whole universe, "When you've seen*
*me you've seen God. When you've seen my actions, heard my*
*words, understood my attitudes, received my thoughts,*
*you are getting an exact representation of who God is."*
*WALT HANSEN*

Suggested Hymns
*Amazing Grace*
*Come Ye Sinners, Poor and Wretched*

**1.** What does it mean to you to be made in God's image? Reflect on the quotation at the beginning of this study by Walt Hansen. Then turn to Exodus 20:1-17. The Ten Commandments help us understand the purpose for which we were created. Think about each commandment and what it reveals about the character of God. Spend some time praising him for his attributes.

Then turn your meditations inward. Analyze your own life in light of each commandment. How well are you reflecting the character of God? Where do you fall short?

**2.** Although we are made in God's image to reflect his character, that image in us is twisted, clouded and distorted by the presence of sin. Scripture tells us so, and our hearts and lives convict us. None of us is exempt. We have all sinned and fall short of the glory of God (Rom 3:23). Read Romans 7:7-23 in light of the Ten Commandments. Can you identify with Paul's frustration?

**3.** Now read Romans 7:21—8:11 and Titus 3:3-8. What similarities do you see in these two passages? Summarize Paul's meditation on the dilemma presented in Romans 7. What is the "transition point" in both passages from the old life to the new?

Have you experienced God's grace and mercy poured out to you in Jesus Christ? If so, your meditations on your sinful state need not and should not end in despair (Rom 7:24), but rather in thanksgiving (Rom 7:25). As Edmund Clowney has remarked, "Prolonged self-examination that does not flee to the Lord for cleansing, pardon and relief forgets the personal presence of the Lord by his Spirit and the purpose of his redeeming grace."

**Further Study**

**1.** The book of Ecclesiastes presents a rather different type of meditation on the meaning of man's existence and the purpose of his creation. As you have time, read through the book, joining in its reflections. Note especially 3:11-12; 12:1, 13-14. Is the end of God's creative work in man really "vanity"? What then is the Preacher really saying?

**2.** Compare Isaiah's experience of being in the presence of God and his thoughts about himself (Is 6:1-10) with Paul's considerations of his anticipated being "with Christ" (Phil 1:19-26). How are their experiences and thoughts similar? How are they different? (Incidentally, the Lord of Is 6 is Jesus; see Jn 12:36-43, especially v. 41.)

# 13
# The Providence of God
## (Part I)

*In him we live and move and have our being.*
ACTS 17:28

Q: What do you understand by the providence of God?
A: The almighty and ever-present power of God whereby
he still upholds, as it were by his own hand, heaven and
earth together with all creatures, and rules in such a way that
leaves and grass, rain and drought, fruitful and
unfruitful years, food and drink, health and sickness, riches
and poverty, and everything else, come to us not by
chance but by his fatherly hand.
*THE HEIDELBERG CATECHISM*

Suggested Hymns
*All Creatures of Our God and King*
*Now Thank We All Our God*

**1.** Not only has God created the world and everything in it;
not only has he redeemed the world through the blood of
Jesus Christ, calling all creation to bow to his lordship; but
God also sustains, upholds, provides for and governs all of
creation. This latter activity of God is called his *providence*.

We can meditate on God's providential care as seen in the
created world around us, in the histories of God's people recorded in Scripture and in our own lives. As we do this our
vision of God will expand, and we can know in a fresh way
the meaning of our Father's love for us.

**2.** Read slowly through Psalm 145. Notice how the psalm
progresses, focusing first on the greatness of God for his
mighty acts (vv. 1-7), then on his grace and mercy (vv. 8-13),
and finally on his goodness and providential care (vv. 14-20).

What do you learn about the objects and scope of God's providence?

**3.** Take note of the use of *all* and *every* in verses 8-21. You may want to underline or circle each occurrence. Can you draw generalizations about these uses? Is there also significant variety that can be noted? What is the impact and meaning of this pattern?

**4.** Verse 5 speaks explicitly of *meditate*. Notice the pattern of the verbs in verses 1-7. What do these verbs have in common? What does this imply about the verb *meditate* and about the experience of meditation?

**5.** Spend some time reflecting on the verbs and phrases in verses 14-20. Think about how God has met or is meeting specific needs in your own life through his providential care.

**6.** How does the psalmist respond to God after meditating on his providence (v. 21)? How will you?

**Further Study**

**1.** Matthew 5:43-48 is a practical illustration of the providence of God. Spend some time reflecting on this passage. How does God show himself to be provident? What benefits can come from meditating on the providence of God?

**2.** Examples of God's providence in the lives of men and women abound in Scripture. Take time today or later this week to read through at least one of the following passages: Genesis 37—50; Ruth 1—4; Esther 1—10; John 17—20; Acts 26—28; 2 Corinthians 6:3-10; 11:1—12:21. Notice how God was actively involved in ways both common and wonderful in the affairs of his people—preserving, governing, upholding, protecting and using for good what was intended for evil.

# 14
# The Providence of God
## (Part II)

*. . . For we are indeed his offspring.*
ACTS 17:28

Q: *What advantage comes from acknowledging God's
creation and providence?*
A: *We learn that we are to be patient in adversity, grateful
in the midst of blessing, and to trust our faithful God and
Father for the future, assured that no creature shall
separate us from his love, since all creatures are so completely in his hand that without his will they
cannot even move.*
THE HEIDELBERG CATECHISM

Suggested Hymns
*God Moves in a Mysterious Way*
*There's a Wideness in God's Mercy*

**1.** Meditating on the providence of God in our lives is meant
to be a stimulus for praise and thanksgiving and a means of
encouraging others as we share our experiences of God's
mercy to us. Read through Psalm 107. As you read about the
various deliverances, think of how God has delivered you in
times of trouble. Pay special attention to verses 1-3, 8, 15,
21-22, 31-32 and 43 for appropriate responses to the providence of God in your life. Let your prayers reflect the attitude
of the psalmist.
**2.** While Psalm 107 focuses on God's providential care over
us, Psalm 104 shows God's governing and sustaining hand
over all creation. As you read Psalm 104, list the activities
by which God works out his providence.

How does God, in his providence, act in similar ways in

your life? Make a note of any instances of God's care for you
that you have taken for granted in the past months. Spend
some time in prayer today thanking God for these things.
**3.** According to the psalmist, Psalm 104 is a meditation (v.
34). Consider the following sections of the psalm to see how
the psalmist structures his meditation.

☐ Verses 1-4:    The number of pronouns and the person to
                 whom they refer is a good clue as to the
                 focus of the psalmist's attention.
☐ Verses 5-9:    The psalmist reaches back to the beginning
                 of time to meditate on God's work.
☐ Verses 10-30:  God provides for and orders all creation.
☐ Verses 31-35:  The psalm begins and ends in a similar way.
                 How are these verses like verses 1-4?

**Further Study**
**1.** Reflecting on our own past history and God's providential
care for us can be a valuable means of integrating our lives.
It enables us to pull together the pieces of our lives into a
meaningful whole. This can make us more aware of our value
and worth to God. The following outline provides you with
some key events to meditate on along with some biblical
references that may help you focus your meditations. As you
meditate today and in the days ahead, consider the advan-
tages that have come to you through the ordering of God's
providence in your life.

☐ My birth and upbringing (Gal 1:11-24).
**1.** My formation and protection in the womb (Ps 139:13-16).
**2.** The place and time of my birth (Ex 1:15—2:10).
☐ My conversion (Eph 2:11-22; Acts 26:9-23).
**1.** The occasion of my conversion (Jn 4).
**2.** The instrument or means of my conversion (Acts 8:26-40).
☐ My employment (Eph 6:5-9).
**1.** Past (Mt 4:18-19).
**2.** Present (Mt 6:33).
☐ My family affairs and relationships (Phil 2:1-4).

**1.** Immediate family (Eph 5:21—6:4).
**2.** The body of Christ (1 Cor 12:12-27).
☐ My safety and preservation from evil (Ps 121; Dan 3; Acts 12:1-17).*

---

\* *Portions of the above outline are from John Flavel,* The Mystery of Providence *(Edinburgh: Banner of Truth, 1976).*

# 15
# The Works of God in History: Redemption

*For whatever was written in former days was written for our instruction, that by steadfastness and by the encouragement of the scriptures we might have hope.*
ROMANS 15:4

*The notion of remembering in Hebrew is more than a calling to mind. It involves a remembering with concern; it also implies loving reflection and, where called for, a corresponding degree of action.*
MARTEN H. WOUDSTRA

Suggested Hymns
*And Can It Be*
*Glorious Things of Thee Are Spoken*
*Rock of Ages*

**1.** The life of the faithful Hebrew was saturated in the remembrance of God's deeds in history. Therefore, it is not surprising to find that his thoughts returned to these remembrances as objects of meditation when faced with difficulties in his own life and faith. An excellent example of this is found in Psalm 77. Read through the entire psalm, noticing the situation of the psalmist. What was his reason for meditating?

**2.** Three times in this psalm *meditate* is used. Consider these usages as found in verses 3, 6 and 12 (the word for *meditate* in v. 3 is often translated "sigh" or "moan"). What other verbs and phrases in the immediate context of each of these three verses are similar in meaning to *meditate*? How do these similarities enrich your idea of meditation?

**3.** The greatest redemptive act of God in the Old Testament was the exodus from Egypt. Did you notice the psalmist's final focus on this event in verses 11-20? Why do you suppose he ends up thinking about the exodus? What changes do you see in the psalmist's concept of God as a result of his meditations on these historical events? Note the imagery throughout these verses, especially comparing verses 7-10 with verse 20. Why did his concept of God change? Of what value were his meditations to his present situation? Compare his "conclusion" in verse 20 to verses 1-2. Did he find an answer or solution to his "trouble"? What was it?

**4.** What situation do you face today that could be similar to that of the meditator in Psalm 77? Think in terms of both your personal life and the world situation. What specific deeds of the Lord can you recall from your personal history and/or the history of God's people recorded in Scripture that would be fruitful objects for your meditations? Meditate on these now in light of current circumstances.

**Further Study**

**1.** How are we as New Testament believers to relate to God's dealings with his chosen people of the Old Covenant? What can we gain by meditating on the works of God in history? First, consider Romans 15:4. Then read Hebrews 10:32—12:2 noting the specific Old Testament scenes which apply to the life of New Testament believers. What message should we get from meditating on these lessons from the past?

**2.** Continue your consideration of the significance of the Old Testament by reading 1 Corinthians 10:1-13. What Old Testament scenes are the believers to remember here?

**3.** Consider the use of the exodus imagery in Psalms 105, 106, 66:5-7 and Isaiah 43:16-21. In each case why is the particular imagery used? How does the imagery vary from passage to passage? Does this variation carry different shades of meaning? You may also want to read the original account in Exodus 12—15.

# 16
# The Word of God

*I have laid up thy word in my heart . . .*
PSALM 119:11

*What is a Christian? He can be described from many angles,
but from what we have said it is clear that we can cover
everything by saying: he is a man who acknowledges and
lives under the word of God. He submits without reserve to
the word of God written in "the Scripture of truth"
(Dan. 10:21), believing the teaching, trusting the promises,
following the commands. His eyes are to the God of the
Bible as his Father, and the Christ of the Bible as his Savior.
He will tell you if you ask him, that the word of God has
both convinced him of sin and assured him of forgiveness. His
conscience, like Luther's, is captive to the word of
God, and he aspires, like the psalmist, to have his whole life
brought into line with it. . . . The promises are before him
as he prays, and the precepts are before him as he
moves among men. He knows that in addition to the word
of God spoken directly to him in the Scriptures, God's
word has also gone forth to create, and control, and order
things around him; but since the Scriptures tell him that all
things work together for his good, the thought of God
ordering his circumstances brings him only joy. He is an
independent fellow, for he uses the word of God as a
touchstone by which to test the various views that are put to
him, and he will not touch anything which he is not sure
that Scripture sanctions.*

*Why does this description fit so few of us who profess
to be Christians in these days? You will find it
profitable to ask your conscience, and let it tell you.*
J. I. PACKER

Suggested Hymns
*According to Thy Gracious Word
How Firm a Foundation
O Word of God Incarnate*

**1.** The Word of God is of utmost importance to our Christian lives. What do you conclude about the purposes of that Word (both Old and New Testaments) from the following verses: Luke 24:25-27; John 5:39-47; 20:30-31? How are the purposes of these verses the same as the purposes for meditating on nature and self? How are they different? Can meditation on only nature or self bring knowledge and belief that Jesus is the Christ?

**2.** What do the following passages say about the source, purpose and ultimate effect of the written Word on our lives: Romans 15:4-6; 2 Timothy 3:16-17? How could these purposes and effects be enhanced in our lives by meditating on Scripture?

**3.** Jesus used Scripture to counter temptation (Lk 4:1-13), define his role in society (Lk 4:16-22) and direct others into the paths of eternal life (Lk 10:25-28). What are some areas in which you would like to see more clearly how Scripture applies to your life? job? studies? relationships with the opposite sex? church? Investigate an area of concern in your own life. Meditate on what Scripture has to say about it. Then resolve and make plans to obey.

**4.** In Psalm 19:1-6 we discovered nature as an object of meditation (see study nine). Read slowly through Psalm 19:7-14. What is the object of the psalmist's meditation here? How would you characterize the psalmist's attitude toward the Word? What effect does the Word have on the whole person (vv. 7-11)? What do the psalmist's meditations on the Word prompt him to do (vv. 11-14)? Why?

**5.** Spend some time reflecting on your own relationship to the written Word of God. How would you describe your own attitude toward the Old Testament? The New?

Have you experienced any of the effects of the Word in your own life similar to the psalmist's in Psalm 19? If so, write down a few.

Does your own attitude and response to the Word of God compare favorably with that of the psalmist/meditator? What changes would you like to make in your life?

**Further Study**
**1.** Work through the Gospel of Luke, or all four Gospels if you prefer, noticing Jesus' attitude toward the Word of God. Make note not only of his statements about God's Word but also his use of the Old Testament. When you have done this, see if his statements can be organized and summarized under general headings.

# 17
# The Promises of God

*For all the promises of God find their Yes in him. That is why we utter the Amen through him, to the glory of God.*
2 CORINTHIANS 1:20

*A fixed, constant attention to the promises, and a firm belief of them, would prevent solicitude and anxiety about the concerns of this life. It would keep the mind quiet and composed in every change, and support and keep up our sinking spirits under the several troubles of life.... Christians deprive themselves of their most solid comforts by their unbelief and forgetfulness of God's promises. For there is no extremity so great, but there are promises suitable to it, and abundantly sufficient for our relief in it.*

*A thorough acquaintance with the promises would be of the greatest advantage in prayer. With what comfort may the Christian address himself to God in Christ when he considers the repeated assurances that his prayers shall be heard! With how much satisfaction may he offer up the several desires of his heart when he reflects upon the texts wherein those very mercies are promised! And with what fervour of spirit and strength of faith may he enforce his prayers, by pleading the several gracious promises which are expressly to his case!*
SAMUEL CLARK

Suggested Hymns
*Go to the Deeps of God's Promise*
*I Heard the Voice of Jesus Say*
*Standing on the Promises*

**1.** In study eight we saw how Mary meditated on the promises of God with great benefit to her life. This study focuses on some promises of God to believers and the value of meditating on these promises for our lives today. Begin by reading

2 Peter 1:3-4. What has been granted to the believer? By what means? What are the benefits? What is the ultimate goal? Are there any sinful situations from which you need to escape? How could meditating on the promises of God help you do this?

**2.** Read James 1:12-15. What trials and temptations are you facing or might you be facing this week? What promise is given in James 1:12? How could meditating on this promise help you endure your trials and resist a specific temptation? (See also Jas 2:5 and Rev 3:10-13.) Apply it to your life today and in the week ahead.

**3.** Read John 14:1-7. Here the disciples are anxious and troubled in spirit, anticipating the death of Jesus and quite possibly their own. Notice the commands Jesus gives the disciples. What present and future promises does Jesus speak of to encourage the disciples concerning each command? How could meditating on these promises be of benefit to you today? in the future? to others you know who might be facing death?

**4.** This study touches on only a few of the hundreds of promises in Scripture. It is meant to introduce you to the potential benefits of a lifetime of meditating on the promises of God. Notice how in each case they are directly related to a specific situation of fear, anxiety, temptation or the like. Meditating on the promises is very practical! The further study section gives some suggestions for a more thorough look at the promises of God in both the Old and New Testaments. Whenever you study the Scriptures you can look for promises God gives to strengthen and encourage your faith and motivate you to live your life in obedience to his will. Remember, most promises do not stand alone. Faith and obedience are prerequisites. Make the promises of God specific objects for your meditations in the days ahead.

**Further Study**

**1.** Scripture abounds with the promises of God graciously given to those who believe. The following references are only a few of those promises. Meditate on them as you have time, savoring God's goodness to you. Perhaps you can begin another list of promises gleaned from your own Scripture reading.

☐ From the Old Testament: Genesis 3:14-19 (especially v. 15); Deuteronomy 28; Numbers 23:19; Isaiah 9:1-7; 41:10; 43:1-3; 65:17-25; Lamentations 3:22-23; Proverbs 3:9-10.

☐ From the New Testament: Matthew 7:7-11; 11:28-30; Luke 18:29-30; John 3:16-18; 14—15; Romans 8:32; 10:10; Philippians 4:19; 2 Peter 3:8-13; 1 John 1:9.

# 18
# The Law of God

*For Christ is the end of the law, that every one who*
*has faith may be justified.*
ROMANS 10:4

*How I love Thy law, O Lord:*
*Daily joy its truths afford;*
*In its constant light I go,*
*Wise to conquer every foe.*

*Sweeter are Thy words to me*
*Than all other good can be;*
*Safe I walk, Thy truth my light,*
*Hating falsehood, loving right.*
*ANONYMOUS*

Suggested Hymns
*How I Love Thy Law, O Lord*
*Let Us Love, and Sing*
*That Man Is Blest Who Fearing God*

**1.** In the very first studies in this book, we saw in both
Psalms 1 and 119 how fundamental the law of God was to
meditation. Now we will turn to a more in-depth study of the
law. Begin by reading Deuteronomy 6:1-9. What does this
passage say about the following?
☐ The origin of the law.
☐ The purpose of the law.
☐ The basic content of the law.
☐ What people are to do with the law.
  Note especially verses 6-9. How might these verses relate
to meditation?
**2.** What do Romans 3:19-20 and Galatians 3:19-26 say about
the law? What does the law show us about our nature? What
results should be evident in our lives if we meditate on God's

law? (See esp. Gal 3:24.)

**3.** Christ says, "Think not that I have come to abolish the law and the prophets; I have come not to abolish them but to fulfil them" (Mt 5:17). One way in which Jesus fulfilled the law was by living in perfect obedience to it. Furthermore, by taking upon himself our sin and the punishment which the law dictates for our disobedience, Jesus fulfilled the negative aspects of the law (cf. 2 Cor 5:21; Gal 3:13-14). How else did Jesus fulfill the law? (As you answer this question, think also about the ways in which the law was inadequate or unfulfilled before the coming of Christ. Consider Rom 8:3-4; Heb 9:6-14, 25-26.)

**4.** Read Matthew 5:17-48. How does Jesus illumine the true meaning of the laws on which he comments? How can our meditations on the law change in light of this passage?

How do Jesus' meditations in these verses provide a model for meditation in general? Consider both his style and content.

**5.** Keeping in mind Deuteronomy 6:4-5, compare Luke 10: 25-28 and Galatians 5:14. How do these New Testament references expand upon the Deuteronomy passage? What should be the result of meditating on the law of God?

**Further Study**

**1.** You may wish to refresh your memory of the various aspects of the law by reviewing the Ten Commandments (Ex 20: 1-17 or Deut 5:1-21) and the specific laws of the covenant (for example, Ex 21—23). The entire book of Leviticus discusses laws and rituals of worship given by God to the Israelites through Moses.

**2.** 1 Corinthians 13 spells out in detail what is involved in the law of love. Take time to meditate on a few of the aspects of love described there. Reflect on *what* the law of love is and *how* it can be applied to specific situations in your life.

# 19
# God Himself

*On the glorious splendor of thy majesty, and on thy*
*wondrous works, I will meditate.*
*PSALM 145:5*

*O Majesty unspeakable, my soul desires to behold Thee. I*
*cry to Thee from the dust.*

*Yet when I inquire after Thy name it is secret. Thou art*
*hidden in the light which no man can approach unto.*
*What Thou art cannot be thought or uttered, for Thy glory*
*is ineffable.*

*Still, prophet and psalmist, apostle and saint have*
*encouraged me to believe that I may in some measure know*
*Thee. Therefore, I pray, whatever of Thyself Thou has*
*been pleased to disclose, help me to search out as treasure*
*more precious than rubies or the merchandise of fine gold;*
*for with Thee shall I live when the stars of the twilight are no*
*more and the heavens have vanished away and only*
*Thou remainest. Amen.*
*A. W. TOZER*

Suggested Hymns
*Holy, Holy, Holy*
*Immortal, Invisible, God Only Wise*
*O Worship the King*

**1.** An attribute of God can be defined as "whatever God has
in any way revealed as being true of himself" (Tozer, *Knowledge of the Holy*, p. 20). In the previous studies we have already reflected on some of God's attributes as he has revealed
them to us in the things he has made and done. Spend a few
minutes thinking back to previous studies. What specific
attributes of God come to mind?
**2.** Read Psalm 145, noticing the focus of the psalmist's meditations in verse 5. What is (are) the object(s) of meditation?

Do you think one or two different objects are mentioned? Why? How do verses 6-13 amplify and clarify the object(s) mentioned in verse 5?

**3.** Reread Psalm 145, listing specific attributes of God the psalmist has discovered. Spend some time thinking about these attributes. What is distinctive about each one? How has God revealed these aspects of his character to you recently?

**4.** Psalm 145 is far from an abstract study. It expresses the heart of personal worship and devotion to God. Note the various responses of the psalmist as he reflects on God's greatness, graciousness and goodness. What does this tell you about the purpose and process of meditating on the attributes and works of God? Also notice the nouns and personal pronouns used to address God. Is there a pattern to this usage? What does this tell you about the psalmist's relationship to God?

**Further Study**
**1.** In both Old and New Testaments, beholding is intimately bound up with meditation (cf. study twenty-six). In some contexts, looking, seeing and inquiring are synonyms for meditating. In Psalms 27:4 and 63:2 these phrases are associated with three specific attributes of God. Read these verses and spend some time thinking about these attributes. Ask God to give you a fresh appreciation for these aspects of his character.

**2.** *Knowing God* by J. I. Packer (IVP) is a good introduction to the attributes of God.

# 20
# Jesus Christ

*Consider Jesus...*
*HEBREWS 3:1*

*If I have observed anything by experience, it is this:*
*a man may take the measure of his growth and decay in grace*
*according to his thoughts and meditations upon the*
*person of Christ, and the glory of Christ's kingdom, and of his love.*
*JOHN OWEN*

Suggested Hymns
*All Hail the Power*
*Fairest Lord Jesus*
*Jesus Shall Reign*
*"Man of Sorrows"*

**1.** In a most special way, Jesus is to be the central object of our meditations. He is the one who makes God known to us (Jn 1:18; 14:7-9). He is the image of his Father (Col 1:15). He is the one in whom all the fullness of God dwells bodily (Col 2:9). He is the one who fully reveals God's glory (2 Cor 3:18; 4:4). He is the creator (Jn 1:3; Heb 1:2), sustainer (Heb 1:3; 1 Cor 1:8) and the culmination of redemptive history (Acts 13: 16-41). He is lord and king (Phil 2:9-10), prophet, high priest and savior (Mt 21:11; Heb 2:17; 4:14; Lk 2:11). In short, Jesus is all in all.

The primary source of our knowledge of Jesus is the Bible. The Old Testament Scriptures point us to the person and work of Christ in history and prophecy, while the Gospel accounts give us a picture of his earthly life and ministry. The

Acts record the early works of the exalted Christ through his Spirit, and the Epistles give instruction and application of his life and work to believers. Revelation teaches us to truly worship the one who shall reign for ever and ever as King of kings and Lord of lords.

**2.** Several New Testament passages which focus on Jesus are hymnlike in nature. Spend some time reading, reciting, meditating on, memorizing, even singing at least one of the following hymns of praise to Christ: John 1:1-14; Philippians 2:1-11; Colossians 1:13-20. You will probably want to return to these passages often.

**3.** A large portion of each Gospel focuses on the passion and resurrection of our Lord (Mt 26—28; Mk 14—16; Lk 19—24; Jn 13—21). Likewise, the early preaching and teaching of the apostles emphasized Christ's death and, more especially, his resurrection (for example, Acts 2:14-36; 13:16-41). We too must realize the centrality of this work of salvation. Consider Isaiah 52:13—53:12, which prophetically records this work of Christ. As you reflect on this passage, meditate on the specific incidents in Christ's passion to which the verses refer.

**4.** In 1 Corinthians 11:24, Paul quotes Christ as commanding us to celebrate Holy Communion in remembrance of him. As we noted in study fifteen, remembering and meditating are very closely bound together. With that in mind, reflect on the Lord's Supper as a sign of Christ's death and resurrection, the death of our old self and our new resurrection life in him, our unity with his body of all believers.

**5.** Christian meditation is unique in that we are transformed through it to become like Christ (2 Cor 3:18). The following passages instruct us in how we are to imitate Christ: John 13:34; Ephesians 5:1-4; Philippians 3:10-11; Colossians 3: 12-15. (See question one in the Further Study below for others.) Choose one of the passages and write down concrete ways in which it could apply to your life. Note the specific ways that we are called to imitate Christ.

**Further Study**
**1.** Examine the following passages which further illumine how we are to imitate Christ: Romans 12:1-2; 1 Corinthians 11:1; Galatians 2:20; Colossians 3:1-2; 1 John 3:1-3.
**2.** We began this study with a quotation from Hebrews. Study the book of Hebrews, underlining or recording each bit of information about Jesus. Notice also what might be considered exhortations to meditate: Hebrews 3:1-6; 12:1-3. Take particular note of the context, the purpose and the expected result of the exhortation.
**3.** Study the letters to the seven churches in Revelation 2—3. Take note of what is said there about Jesus.
**4.** Study the development of the Old Testament understanding of the messianic types such as Isaac, Jonah and David.
**5.** Meditate on the various names of Jesus used throughout the Bible, such as: Immanuel (Is 7:14), the Word (Jn 1:1; Rev 19:13), Son of God (Jn 3:18; 5:25), Son of Man (Mt 8:20; 9:6), the Righteous One (Is 53:11; Acts 7:52), Lord (i.e., Yahweh or Jehovah; cf. Rom 10:9-13 with Joel 2:32). See also Matthew 27:1; Acts 2:27; 1 Corinthians 2:8; Revelation 20:16; 21:22 and 22:12-13.

# III
# Images
# of
# Meditation

Throughout the Bible we encounter colorful, picturesque language that helps us see and understand more clearly what is being communicated. Often a Western, rational, scientific mind would rather skip over such language, preferring the closely reasoned thinking of writers such as Paul. Yet God in his wisdom and love has chosen to reveal himself to us using the whole range of verbal expression—the psalms (or songs), the prophetic writings, historical narration in both Old and New Testaments, the letters to churches and so on.

Figures of speech or images, as we have loosely called them, are probably most obvious in Jesus' parables. Christ also creates vivid images through such phrases as "I am the door" and "I am the true vine." The prophets frequently use imagery in an effort to communicate to the wayward nation of Israel. Even Paul uses this kind of language. For example, he compares Israel to a cultivated olive tree and the Gentiles to a wild branch grafted into it (Rom 11:17-24).

In this part we will not simply study images in general, or even images which through the years have been particularly rewarding to others, such as the pastoral imagery of Psalm 23. We will study that imagery or figurative language which describes meditation or the meditative process. Thus we will continue to seek what the Bible says about meditation.

Getting dressed, eating at a feast, being a servant—these are the kinds of images which this section explores because they are the images of meditation given to us in the Bible. They are not the graven images whose worship the second commandment expressly forbids. They are figures of speech, not of our invention but given by God in his Word. In studying these divinely given illustrations we simply desire to understand and heed God's teaching.

The images of meditation presented in Scripture provide us with much useful information. We are probably used to thinking of an image as a vague picture in the mind, rather than a valuable resource for information. We want you to grow more self-conscious about this style of learning so that you can go more deeply into the truth, and so that Scripture can go more deeply into you.

# 21
# Tree

*Blessed is the man who trusts in the LORD, whose trust is the
LORD. He is like a tree planted by water, that sends out
its roots by the stream, and does not fear when heat comes,
for its leaves remain green, and is not anxious in the
year of drought, for it does not cease to bear fruit.*
*JEREMIAH 17:7-8*

*Thought when nourished by meditation is like the tree
which, in proportion as it grows higher and spreads its
branches wider, in quest of air and light, strikes its roots ever
deeper and multiplies incessantly the thousand shoots
which reach out in the surrounding earth to get more nourishment and to gain new resisting power against the pressure
of the winds above.*
*JOSEPH McSORLEY*

Suggested Hymns
*That Man Is Blest Who Fearing God*
*Blessed Is the Man*

**1.** We have already seen in the first study that the person
who meditates is likened to a tree. Read again Psalm 1:1-3
to reconsider the image of the tree. What three verbs are used
in verse 3 to describe the tree? What qualifying statement is
associated with each verb? How does the man of verses 1 and 2
resemble a tree? Look especially at the last sentence of verse 3.
**2.** Turn now to Jeremiah 17:7-8. Jeremiah is thought to have
picked up the image of Psalm 1:3. What similarities and differences do you recognize? How do the differences clarify
and illumine your understanding and enrich your appreciation of this image?
**3.** Now that you have meditated on this image of the tree,
bring together your thoughts on how this image develops
your understanding of meditation. Remember—it is the one

who meditates on God's law who is like the tree (Ps 1:2).
**4.** Various aspects of this tree image are used elsewhere in Scripture. For example, read John 15:1-11 where a similar agricultural image is used. What similarities do you see between the vine and the tree? What does John 15 say about "bearing fruit" (cf. vv. 2, 4-5)? What is the means or source of bearing fruit here? in Psalm 1? in Jeremiah 17? What is the purpose of bearing fruit in John 15? What type of fruit is in view here? (Gal 5:22 may shed further light on this question.)
**5.** A second aspect of the tree image is the root (cf. Jer 17:8). Read Matthew 13:1-23. What agricultural image is used in this parable? What is the importance of the root in this image (cf. vv. 5, 21)? How is it that the seed of the Word of God takes root and bears fruit in our lives (cf. vv. 19, 23)? How is this related to meditation? (Keep in mind Ps 1:1-3 and Jer 17:7-8 as you answer this last question.)
**6.** Don't forget to use trees in nature as objects for meditation. Such meditation, together with scriptural insight, can prove enjoyable and rewarding. (See Ps 104:10-23 for examples of meditations on various aspects of the tree image.)

**Further Study**
**1.** Consider the following aspects of the tree image as developed elsewhere in Scripture: being planted (Is 61:1-4; Jas 1:21), streams of water (Ps 46:4; Ezek 47:12; Jn 7:37; Rev 22:2), leaves (Is 64:6; Rev 22:2), agricultural growth (Mt 13:31-32; 1 Cor 6—9). Consider also, pruning (Jn 15:2, 6) and grafting (Rom 11:17-36).
**2.** Consider the imagery of Ephesians 4:14-21 (esp. v. 17) for its import regarding the tree imagery and meditation.
**3.** How does the "abiding" language of John 15:1-11 enrich your understanding of meditation?
**4.** The following tree imagery provides much fruit for meditation!
☐ Israel considered as a forest being cut down and burned for its sin (Is 10:15-19, 33-34—note how John the Baptist echoes

this language of judgment as he prepares the way for Christ in Mt 3:8-10).

☐ Christ, a shoot springing up from the stump of Jesse (Is 11: 1-3, 10; 53:1-2).

☐ The righteousness which God will give to his people (Is 45: 8; 51:3; 61:11).

# 22
# Feasting

*Thy words were found, and I ate them,*
*and thy words became to me a joy*
*and the delight of my heart;*
*for I am called by thy name,*
*O LORD, God of hosts.*
JEREMIAH 15:16

*As one that is either weary or weak recovereth strength by*
*taking his food, although he eateth many times without*
*either appetite or taste; so meditation and prayer, which give*
*both fuel and flame unto devotion, do increase in us some*
*spiritual strength, even when they yield little spiritual solace.*
H. HAYWOOD

Suggested Hymns
*Break Thou the Bread of Life*
*Here, O My Lord, I See Thee Face to Face*
*Jesus, Thou Joy of Loving Hearts*

**1.** Psalm 63, which speaks of the soul as thirsting after God and later being satisfied as if richly fed, refers explicitly to meditation in verse 6. (This psalm is studied in more detail in Further Study below.) If you have not already thought about meditation as an experience of feasting, spend some time now reflecting on this image. Do you hunger after God and his Word? How would you describe your enjoyment of a good meal? Would you be able to describe your times of meditation in a similar way?

**2.** The following passages, while not explicitly about meditation, all speak of eating and/or drinking: Jeremiah 15:16; Psalm 19:7-10; John 4:7-15, 32-34; 6:35; 1 Peter 2:2-3. For each of these passages, consider the following questions:

☐ How are the specific foods and beverages (or just food and drink in general) like the object to which they are compared? How, for example, is Jesus like bread (Jn 6:35)?

☐ Which of these foods have we seen previously as the objects of meditation?

☐ What does the eating and drinking of the soul involve? How is it described? In what ways is it similar to the process of meditation?

☐ What results are anticipated through the partaking of this spiritual food or drink? How do they compare to the results of meditation?

**3.** Analyze your own eating patterns and habits. How many times a day do you eat? What types of foods are part of your diet? Why? What are your attitudes toward preparing for meals? Are you satisfied with when you eat and what you eat? Do you need to change any patterns? Now ask those same questions again in regard to your spiritual nourishment through meditation.

**Further Study**

**1.** Read Psalm 63. Where is meditation explicitly spoken of? What other words or phrases in the psalm do you associate with meditation? What mental pictures come to mind as you reflect on verse 1? Have you ever experienced your soul thirsting or your flesh fainting for someone or something? for God? Recapture your experience in words and feelings.

**2.** What image or figure used in verse 5 contrasts with the image of verse 1? Think about the meaning of a feast. Reflect on various feasts you have enjoyed—for example, Thanksgiving or Christmas dinners, at weddings, birthdays or anniversary celebrations. In what ways are some of these experiences analogous to meditation? Think about the phrase "my soul is feasted as with marrow and fatness." What are marrow and fat like in meditation?

**3.** In Psalm 63 what intervenes in the experience of the psalmist to account for the changed imagery between verses 1 and 5? How do these situations relate to meditation? See especially verses 2, 6-8.

**4.** Feasting is generally thought of as taking in food and drink. In Psalm 63 the image of feasting also includes giving out. According to verse 5, what does feasting involve that adds to your understanding of the meditative process?

# 23
# Dressing

*Put off your old nature ... be renewed in the spirit of your minds ... put on the new nature, created after the likeness of God in true righteousness and holiness.*
EPHESIANS 4:22-24

*Jesus, thy blood and righteousness*
*My beauty are, my glorious dress*
*Midst flaming worlds, in these arrayed,*
*With joy shall I lift up my head.*
NICHOLAS VON ZINZENDORF

Suggested Hymn
*Jesus, Thy Blood and Righteousness*

**1.** While biblical imagery involving clothing is probably not new to most, its use with regard to meditation may be unfamiliar. This study is devoted to a particular aspect of clothing—taking it off and putting it on! In the same way that our clothing is often a reflection of who we are, so the things we clothe our minds and actions in show what we are really like. More than that, our mental clothes help create who we are and what we do.

**2.** Read Colossians 3:1-17. This passage introduces the clothing image between two other expressions which more obviously deal with meditation—setting your mind (vv. 1-2) and letting "the word of Christ dwell in you richly" (v. 16). Describe the use of clothing imagery in this passage. Consider first the negative side, the "putting off" of verses

2, 5, 8 and 9. What is the relationship between this and the negative aspect of meditation—the things which we are *not* to set our minds on? Next consider the positive side, the "putting on" of verses 10, 12 and 14. How is it related to the things which we *are* to set our minds on? Also, how is this positive side related to the Word of Christ dwelling within (v. 16)?

Meditate on these verses until you are able to decide whether you agree that the clothing image (put off/put on) is intimately involved with meditation.

**3.** Ephesians 4:17—5:21 is similar in many ways to Colossians 3:1-17. Read the Ephesians passage, noting especially the investiture language in 4:22, 24 and 25. What similarities and differences are there with the Colossians 3 passage? Notice also the similarities between Ephesians 5:18-21 and Colossians 3:15-17. Both of these passages contain many specific and practical directives on "how one ought to behave in the household of God" (1 Tim 3:15). Make a note of any particulars which are especially applicable to yourself. Do you bear a grudge instead of laying aside your anger? Are all your words good for building up, or do they often tear down? Are you really tenderhearted to _____ ? Your meditation should actually involve a putting off or putting on in accordance with what is written in these passages.

**4.** Do the godly meditations of the new person in Christ govern your actions? Reflect on your life since the first studies you did on meditation until now. How have your actions been influenced by your meditations?

**5.** You may want to consider your daily times of dressing as a time to meditate in preparation for the events to come. Just as you would not want to go out without dressing your body, so you should not want to go out into a new day without dressing your soul. Your times of quiet meditation before God and his Word can be just such times of preparation too.

**Further Study**
**1.** Between the "putting off" of Ephesians 4:22 and the

"putting on" of Ephesians 4:24, what intervenes in Ephesians 4:23? This seems to be the pivotal point in the investiture process—the renewal of the inner person which is the ultimate goal of biblical meditation. Notice the idea of renewal in Colossians 3:10, 2 Corinthians 4:16 (both closely related to clothing; cf. also 2 Cor 5:2-5), 2 Corinthians 3:18 and Romans 12:1-2. Note, however, that the renewal will not be completed simply by meditation. Consider Colossians 3:1-4, 1 John 3:1-3, 1 Corinthians 15:50-57, 1 Thessalonians 4:15-17.

**2.** Consider the clothing instructions—both internal and external—given to wives in 1 Peter 3:1-6. How does this language remind you of meditation?

**3.** Consider the following passages:

☐ Galatians 3:27. How is the clothing image used here? What is put on? Who is responsible for the putting on? What are the implications of this investiture (cf. vv. 23-27)?

☐ Romans 13:12, 14. What is put on in these verses? What behavior should follow? It is wise to consider these verses in their broader context.

☐ 1 Corinthians 15:53-54. What is being put on here? What are these verses describing (cf. vv. 51-57)? When is the time of this putting on? How does this "when" bear on your present meditations?

Don't be surprised if some difficulties arise in the coordinating and integrating of these various usages of getting dressed. Time and consistent meditation on these verses is needed for a full understanding.

**4.** *The Centrality of the Resurrection* by Richard B. Gaffin and *Images of the Spirit* by Meredith Kline (both from Baker Book House, Grand Rapids) offer further insight into the investiture image.

# 24
# Servant
## (Part I)

*This book of the law shall not depart out of your mouth, but*
*you shall meditate on it day and night, that you may*
*be careful to do according to all that is written in it; for then*
*you shall make your way prosperous, and then you shall*
*have good success.*
*JOSHUA 1:8*

*His [Joshua's] mind was to be exercised upon God's Word*
*with a specific purpose and practical end: not simply to rest*
*in contemplation, but in order to be regulated by its*
*precepts, through a serious inculcating of them upon his*
*heart. Meditation was not to be an occasional luxury,*
*but the regular discharge of a constant duty—"day and night"*
*—and this in order to [develop] a prompter, fuller and*
*more acceptable obedience.*
*ARTHUR W. PINK*

Suggested Hymns
*Lead on, O King Eternal*
*Take My Life, and Let It Be*
*Trust and Obey*

**1.** Obedience is a concept closely tied to meditation in Scripture. Biblical meditation is concerned not only with inner contemplation but also outer conformity of life—both in speech and in action—to that which God has given for meditation.

Look again at Joshua 1:1-9. How is Joshua characterized in verse 1? What is he told to do in verses 7 and 8? Who tells him?

When we read through the book of Joshua to see how this command in verses 2-9 was lived out by Joshua, we find an interesting pattern. Examine the following verses: Joshua 4: 1-10, 15-18; 5:2-3; 8:1-3. What is emphasized in these passages? What do you conclude about the character of Joshua? What is concluded about Joshua in 24:29? What was the effect of Joshua's obedient service to God on the people of Israel (see 24:31)?

Pause now to relate this brief study of Joshua to meditation as it was commanded in Joshua 1:1-9. (Don't cheat; take time to meditate!) Can you relate each of your answers above to the idea and practice of meditation?

**2.** James is also quite concerned that meditation result in effective service. Read James 1:19-27. Even though the word *meditate* is not used in this passage, how does James describe the process of meditation? What is the special object of meditation mentioned (vv. 21, 25)? How is the "meditator" involved in this process (vv. 19, 21-22, 25)? Note the special emphasis on doing in verses 22-25. What are some of the specifics of this obedience as mentioned in verses 26 and 27?

Do your meditations result in the quality of speech (v. 26) and actions (v. 27) expected of the truly religious person?

**3.** It is clear in both Joshua and James that obedience is an integral part of biblical meditation. One image of obedience given in Scripture is that of the servant. This image tells us much about meditation as an outward expression of inner attitudes.

Look first at Psalm 123. Notice the two comparisons given in verse 2. What activity characterizes these servants? What is the point of the comparison? What is it about this activity which further clarifies your understanding of meditation?

We will look at this in more detail in study twenty-six, but for now ask yourself, "Do I meditate in this way?" Perhaps as you notice the ways in which you look, you will also notice how, when and on what you meditate.

**Further Study**

**1.** Examine the parallelism in Joshua 1:7-8. What is common

to these two verses? What is different? What does *meditate* in
verse 8 correspond to in verse 7?

**2.** Study the book of Joshua further for insight into the character of Joshua and the characteristics of meditation. Note
for example the close relationship between God and Joshua,
as indicated in chapter 10, especially verses 10-14.

**3.** Note the figures or images used in James 1:21. How do
these relate to the other figures of meditation introduced in
the previous studies?

**4.** Read Philippians 2:1-13, meditating on the ways in which
Christ exemplified servanthood. How can you adapt your
attitudes and lifestyle to reflect more nearly the example
given by Christ?

# 25
# Servant
## (Part II)

*Come to me, all who labor and are heavy laden, and I will*
*give you rest. Take my yoke upon you, and learn from me; for*
*I am gentle and lowly in heart, and you will find rest*
*for your souls.*
MATTHEW 11:28-29

*Meditation upon the Word of God is one of the most*
*important of all the means of grace and growth in spirituality,*
*yea there can be no true progress in vital and practical*
*godliness without it. Meditation on Divine things is not*
*optional but obligatory, for it is something which*
God has commanded us to attend unto.... This plea "I am
*too busy to engage in regular and spiritual meditation"*
*is an idle excuse, yea it is worse–it is a deceit of your evil*
*heart. It is not because you are short of time, but because*
*you lack a heart for the things of God!... That which*
*most occupies our heart will most engage the mind, for our*
*thoughts always follow our affections: consequently*
*the smallest actions, when we have no delight in them, are*
*tedious and burdensome.*
ARTHUR W. PINK

Suggested Hymns
*All for Jesus*
*May the Mind of Christ My Savior*
*Who Is on the Lord's Side?*

---

**1.** Have you ever had a job where you had to work all night?
Remember (or imagine) how it felt as the night wore on—
and you wore out! You probably felt like the watchman in
Psalm 130. Read this psalm. What activities is he engaged in?
Why is the soul of the psalmist compared to a watchman?
Why was the psalmist waiting, and what did he wait for?
How is the watchman like the servants in Psalm 123? How is

the experience of this servant, the watchman, like meditation? Consider both the particulars of the watchman image
and the context of Psalm 130.

**2.** Waiting—which has several senses—characterizes the
duties of many servants. What two senses of waiting characterize Mary and Martha in Luke 10:38-42? Which sense has
the priority in this situation?

   With whom do you identify the most? What does this say
to you about your Christian life? What changes, if any, do
you need to make? Resolve now to make these.

   Would you say that either Mary or Martha (or both) was
meditating? If so, what characterizes meditation in this passage? If not, why not?

**3.** You may experience waiting in your own life—perhaps for
a bus, or for a friend or opportunity, or for the fulfillment of
some dream or aspiration. What is it about your waiting that is
meditation? Do you focus on an object? Are you open to receive? Do you direct your life around the object of expectation?
Are you ready to respond when the hoped-for object arrives?
What is different about your waiting and your meditating?

**4.** As we meditate before the Lord as obedient servants, beholding his glory and listening to his instruction, we will
want not only to praise God for the beauty of his glory and the
wonder of his wisdom, but also to make plans to live out what
he says in a manner pleasing to him. Notice what Proverbs
16:1 and 16:9 say about our plans. In both word (v. 1) and deed
(v. 9), we are dependent on God to fulfill his will for our lives.
This is what it means to be dependent on the grace of God.
Proverbs 16:3, however, provides the missing link between
verses 1 and 9, and testifies to our dependence upon God.
What does Proverbs 16:3 mean to you? Are there any plans
which you need to submit to God's sovereignty? How is your
attitude like and not like the one expressed in this proverb?

**Further Study**
**1.** Many places throughout the New Testament give specific

commands to those who want to serve the Lord. By meditating on these commands we find out how to live our faith in obedience. Remember that the obedient servant is an image for the one who meditates and that our response in action can be considered part of our meditations (cf. Ps 1; Josh 4:1-10, 15-18; 5:2-3; Jas 1:19-27). Consider the following passages, noting where obedience is called for in specific situations in your life: Matthew 5—7, Ephesians 4—6, Colossians 3—4.

**2.** Several passages in Isaiah have been called the Servant Songs. These songs are usually taken as prophetic descriptions of the Messiah who was promised to God's people. Meditate on one or more of these songs, noticing what characterizes the servant of the Lord and how you should be more like this servant. These songs are found in Isaiah 42:1-9; 49: 1-6; 50:4-11 and 52:13—53:12.

**3.** What contribution does Psalm 127 (esp. vv. 1-2) make to your understanding of the watchman? of meditation?

**4.** What further insight into meditation do Proverbs 19:21 and 20:5, 18 offer?

**5.** Consider what the following passages say about waiting and the benefits promised to those who wait: Psalm 25 (esp. vv. 3, 5, 21); Psalm 27:14; Psalm 37 (esp. vv. 7, 9, 34); Psalm 119 (esp. vv. 43, 74, 81, 114, 147); Isaiah 40:31. In some translations "wait" is alternately rendered "hope." What new sense is added by this variation?

# 26
# Beholding

*So I have looked upon thee in the sanctuary,*
*beholding thy power and glory.*
PSALM 63:2

*The devil cannot take from the soul the light of faith: he,*
*however, removes the light of consideration; so that*
*the soul may not reflect on what it believes. And as it is of no*
*avail to open the eyes in the dark, so says St. Augustine,*
*"it is of no advantage to be near the light if the eyes*
*are closed." The eternal maxims, considered in the light of*
*faith, are most clear; yet if we do not open the eyes of the*
*mind by meditating on them, we live as if we were perfectly*
*blind; and so precipitate ourselves into every vice.*
IGNATIUS

Suggested Hymns
*Eternal Light, Eternal Light*
*Turn Your Eyes upon Jesus*
*When I Survey the Wondrous Cross*

**1.** In the previous two studies we have explored the images of watchmen waiting for the dawn and the maid looking attentively to her mistress. While meditation does involve the expectant longing and looking of these servants, it does not stop there. There is also fulfillment of these desires as we behold the object of our meditations. Look at Psalm 27:4. Note the parallelism among the three final parts of this verse. Some versions of the Bible may translate *meditate* as "inquire." How do these parallels illuminate the meaning of *behold*? What is the psalmist meditating on?

**2.** Read Psalm 63:1-2. How is the psalmist's experience similar to the servant's of the previous studies? How is it different? How do you suppose the beholding of verse 2 is related to the meditating of verse 6?

**3.** The image of beholding God's glory is developed by Paul in 2 Corinthians 3. Looking especially at verse 18, what is the effect of this beholding? This is the same type of experience as recorded in Psalms 27:4 and 63:2, and thus it is a New Testament example of meditation. Have you experienced the glory of the Lord in this way? Read on in 2 Corinthians 4:1-6 for a development of this theme. You may want to pray with the psalmist, "Open my eyes, that I may behold wondrous things out of thy law" (119:18).

**Further Study**
**1.** We behold the glory of God when we meditate on nature too. How is this so in Psalm 19? Compare this with Psalm 8. How might you meditate on the handiwork of God?
**2.** Consider Psalm 17:15 and John 17:24 in light of the discussion and questions above.
**3.** Compare the looking of 2 Corinthians 3:18 with the looking of 2 Corinthians 4:18. Notice how the contrast between transient and eternal is illustrated by the dwelling and clothing images in 2 Corinthians 5. What does 5:7 tell you about the looking of 3:18 and 4:18?
**4.** The object of the meditative gaze has been referred to as "beautiful," "glorious." If it is not clear to you what this experience is, you may want to go to an art museum where objects of beauty are displayed. Observe these works, and observe yourself observing. Such aesthetic experiences are like meditative beholding. Listening to music is a similar experience of meditative hearing.

# 27
# Treasuring

*O the depth of the riches and wisdom and knowledge of God!
How unsearchable are his judgments and how inscrutable
his ways!*
ROMANS 11:33

*Because God is the source of all wisdom, man looks in vain for
wisdom apart from him. Job describes man's search for
understanding as a mining expedition. He may dig out rubies,
sapphires, and gold, but no mine will yield the ore of wisdom
(Job 28). No, "the fear of the Lord, that is wisdom."*
EDMUND P. CLOWNEY

Suggested Hymns
*Fairest Lord Jesus*
*Jesus, Priceless Treasure*
*O the Deep, Deep Love of Jesus*

**1.** We noted from Proverbs 2 (study four) that to "treasure within you" is a variant for meditation. Wisdom and understanding are seen not only as objects which are meditated upon, but as the fruits of meditation (cf. Ps 49 and Prov 8:19). Object or fruit, wisdom is of great worth, even more valuable than silver and gold. Look again at Proverbs 2:1-5 to see how treasuring within can be seen as meditating.

**2.** Psalm 119:11 further substantiates this point. Why does the psalmist "treasure" God's Word? (The Hebrew word here can be translated "to cover, hide" or "to lay in, treasure up, hoard.") How is verse 11 related to the question of verse 9? to the prayer of verse 10b? Would you consider any of the expressions in verses 9-16 as parallel to "treasure in my heart" in verse 11? Especially consider verses 15-16.

3. Pause to consider what you value. Perhaps a ring, a watch or a stereo set; maybe a book, a letter or money. Are there people who are especially valuable to you? How are your relationships with these persons or things different from your relations to others? The following verses give some insight into the psychology of valuing: Psalm 119:14; Proverbs 2:4; 3:15. Amplify these insights from your own experience.

4. You may have noticed (as in Prov 2:4) that seeking is often closely related to the meditation experience. Sometimes the word *seek* is used, as in Psalms 63:1 and 77:2. Other times the seeking is expressed in terms of desire, such as "hungering" and "thirsting" in Psalms 63:1 and 143:6. Occasionally, the seeking is acted out, as in Psalms 77:2; 143:5 and 119:48. From what we have seen in Proverbs 2:4, it is natural to seek after what we consider valuable. Do you find yourself seeking after what you value? What do you seek after?

Jesus said, "Where your treasure is, there will your heart be also" (Mt 6:21). What we seek after is a good indication of where our heart is. As you meditate before God, you will have opportunity to evaluate and perhaps reorder your priorities. What reordering does Jesus suggest in Matthew 6:19-34?

5. The image of the treasuring of something valuable gives rise to another closely related image. Since meditation is likened to treasuring and seeking after silver and gold, the process of mining these precious metals might provide insight into the process of meditation. Those who value silver and gold seek it out, going deep into the earth or a mountain, or patiently sifting for the metal beside a stream or river. Certainly much of greatest value in the Bible is "beneath the surface" and can be obtained only with patience and hard work. We must dig deep to mine the riches of biblical revelation.

Paul was well aware of this. Read Romans 11:33-36. Paul had been struggling with the very difficult and "deep" truth concerning the election of God's people, especially those within the nation of Israel. What is Paul's response to this truth (v. 36)? In 1 Corinthians 2:6-16 he gives further instruction on this same point. To whom are the deep things of God revealed (cf. also 3:1-3)? By whom is this done (2:10, 13)? For what purpose (2:12)?

**Further Study**
**1.** What does God consider valuable? Use a concordance (or collect material from your own Scripture reading) and study passages referring to "treasure," "riches" and "precious."
**2.** One aspect of the mining process is the refinement of the crude metal brought up from the depths. Consider Malachi 3:1-6; 1 Peter 1:6-9; 4:12-19. Using a concordance, study "purify" as seen, for example, in 1 Peter 1:22 and 1 John 3:3. Those who are theologically minded may want to study this doctrine (sanctification) further by consulting various theological texts.
**3.** Imaginative Christian writers have not overlooked this image. In George MacDonald's children's fantasies, Curdie is the miner's son. In J. R. R. Tolkien, the dwarves are miners. Many beautiful passages can be found in their works which enrich our own experience and understanding of mining and thus, indirectly, of meditation.
**4.** Reflect on Matthew 13:44.

# 28
# Dwelling

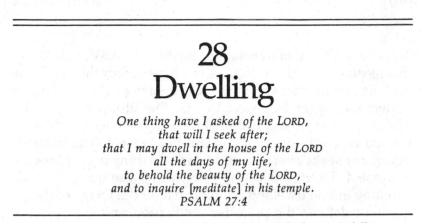

One thing have I asked of the LORD,
that will I seek after;
that I may dwell in the house of the LORD
all the days of my life,
to behold the beauty of the LORD,
and to inquire [meditate] in his temple.
PSALM 27:4

One moment so spent—with the windows of the heart set fully
open toward the heavenly temple, so that the light, and
the air, and the warmth of the very city of God may reach it in
its inmost corners and recesses—is so full of hope, so full
of promise, yea, so full of blessedness, that it makes a man
say, as he retires from it—"Behold, the Lord is in this place, and
I knew it not! This is none other than the house of God,
and this is the gate of heaven!"
DR. C. J. VAUGHAN

Suggested Hymns
*Abide with Me*
*Glorious Things of Thee Are Spoken*
*My Hope Is Built on Nothing Less*
*The Church's One Foundation*

---

**1.** Read Colossians 3:15-17. Although the word *meditate* is not present, it has been suggested (study twenty-three) that the rich indwelling of the Word of Christ (v. 16) is the same idea expressed in different words. Do you find similarities between the concept of meditation in this passage and that developed in earlier studies? What does Colossians 3:15-17 add to that concept?

**2.** *To dwell on* means to repeat or linger over in thought or speech. *To dwell in* means to reside, make one's home, to abide, to remain. Read Psalm 27:4, noting the various aspects of dwelling. The word translated "inquire" (RSV, KJV) and "seek" (NIV) is also translated "meditate" (ASV, NASB). In this psalm as in others, figures or images from the life of the psalmist are interwoven in the text to give a fuller and richer understanding and appreciation of the situation. In Psalm 27:4 the primary image is that of dwelling. Notice the declarative statement in the first two lines of verse 4. The psalmist asks for or seeks after one thing and one thing only. Lines 3-6 of verse 4 describe that one thing using the image of both dwelling in and dwelling on. Notice how the image of dwelling both defines the place for meditation and the object of the meditation. Notice also that the house of the Lord and his temple are parallel phrases. In the Old Testament the glory of the Lord dwelt in the temple of the people of Israel. This glory was called *shekinah glory* or simply *shekinah*, taken from the Hebrew word meaning "dwell, abide, remain." So God is truly not only the object of the psalmist's meditations but, as we will see in later references, his actual dwelling place. Spend time assimilating these insights.

**3.** Reflect on your own experience with various dwelling places. Think about where you live now or the place where you grew up. What is the place you call home? What thoughts and feelings are associated with those places? Does God seem more or less of a home to you than those places?

**4.** Read Deuteronomy 33:26-29 and Psalm 91:1-10. How do the images of dwelling presented in these verses enrich your idea of dwelling? If you are willing to grant that dwelling can be a figurative expression for meditating, which aspects of dwelling enrich your understanding of meditation? How are you enriched?

**5.** John 17:20-24 is an expression of fulfilled dwelling, the consummation of all the images. The word *dwell* is not used directly, but the image is there nevertheless. Spend some time meditating on each verse and phrase. Notice how the image of dwelling develops into knowing, a word that describes the most intimate form of physical, emotional and spiritual union. The image of dwelling then is another way of expressing our union and communion with God as he lives in us through his Holy Spirit and we in him (cf. Rom 8:1-11; Rev 21:3-4, 22). What should be the results of your dwelling or abiding in Christ and Christ in you?

**Further Study**
**1.** Let your thoughts drift to images of castles, cottages, cabins, attics, basements, closets, tents, caves. What do they have in common? How do they differ? How would you feel about living in any of these dwelling places? Why? Spend some time reflecting on the meaning of God as your dwelling place.
**2.** Read John 15:1-11. What synonym for dwelling is used? How does this passage add to your understanding of dwelling? of meditation?
**3.** Often we spend little time meditating on our future heavenly dwelling place. Why do you think this is so? Read John 14:1-11, 2 Corinthians 5:1-5, 1 Thessalonians 4:13-18 and Revelation 21:1—22:5 (esp. 22:1-5). How does meditation on these passages increase your understanding of heaven? How could meditation in general increase your longing for that dwelling place?
**4.** Not only is God himself to be our dwelling place, but the Christian is the dwelling place of God. God's presence, his glory, is no longer confined to the temple. It is in us! Spend some time reflecting on the following passages: Ephesians 2:19-22; 1 Corinthians 6:19-20; 1 Peter 2:4-5; Hebrews 3:5-6. What does the expanded image of ourselves as God's dwelling place say to you about meditation? the things we should both dwell in and on?

# IV
# Principles
# of
# Meditation

*Having looked generally at meditation, at the objects of medita-*
*tion and at images of meditation, we now turn to some specific*
*principles. By looking at the biblical examples and teaching of*
*meditation, we find various patterns which can guide our own*
*understanding and practice. Approaching meditation in this way*
*will help to highlight various distinctives of biblical meditation*
*and encourage us in areas where we may be weak or unclear.*
*Obviously, the whole experience of meditation is greater than*
*any simple sum of its parts. Yet a knowledge of the parts and prin-*
*ciples can certainly assist us in our appreciation for the whole as*
*well as our full participation in its richness.*

# 29
# Centering

*Whom have I in heaven but thee?*
*And there is nothing upon earth that I desire besides thee.*
*PSALM 73:25*

*None other Lamb, none other Name,*
*None other Hope in heav'n or earth or sea,*
*None other hiding place from guilt and shame,*
*None beside Thee.*
*CHRISTINA G. ROSSETTI*

Suggested Hymns
*None Other Lamb*
*Take My Life, and Let It Be*

**1.** Common to virtually all forms of meditation is the centering of oneself, the integration and organization of all that one is on some single object, thought or reference point. Scripture clearly teaches this principle.

In Psalm 103 the psalmist meditates by remembering and recounting God's mercies. Reflect on the first verse of this psalm. How does the phrase "all that is within me" relate to the concept of centering? What do you think the psalmist means by the statement? Read the rest of the psalm for clues. What specifically does the psalmist center his life around? How does he do this? For what reasons? To what end?

**2.** Not only the inner life, however, is involved in biblical meditation. Review Psalm 77. How is the psalmist totally involved in the process of meditation? What activities is he engaged in during his meditations? How do these activities reflect the single concern of the psalmist?

**3.** Read Psalm 27:1-4. What is the situation of the psalmist (vv. 2-3)? In verse 4 the psalmist has centered his desires and now seeks fulfillment. What does he desire to be the focus of his life? What does he want to do? Where does he want to be? How does this verse reflect the wholistic (inner and outer) involvement of the psalmist? How might the situation of verses 2-3 contribute to the affirmations of verses 1 and 4? Are you involved in any analogous situations? In what practical ways could you respond that would be in keeping with verse 4?

### Further Study

**1.** In Psalm 73 we find another illustration of focusing or centering. Initially the psalmist is tempted to envy the prosperity of the wicked who serve mammon (cf. Mt 6:19-24). Read through the entire psalm, noting the conclusions the psalmist comes to about the wicked and how he arrives at those conclusions (vv. 15-20). What do these verses have to do with centering?

Now turn your attention to verses 25-26. What is the focus of the psalmist's meditations here? How is the natural integration of the inner and outer evidenced? How closely do these words express your own heart's desire, the goal of your life and the object of your meditations?

**2.** Read through Psalm 62 noticing the words or phrases that relate to meditation and centering. What is the psalmist's focus? What does the psalmist conclude are the benefits of this centered meditation?

**3.** How is meditation implicit in Matthew 6:19-34? (Review study seven.) How is single-mindedness or focused attention woven into this passage? What new insights does this offer for meditation?

# 30
# The Inner Life
## (Part I)

*I commune with my heart in the night;*
*I meditate and search my spirit.*
*PSALM 77:6*

*Meditation is an inward secret duty; the soul retires into its*
*closet, and bids farewell to the world. It is an invisible*
*duty to the eye of man; and therefore carnal persons do not*
*relish it. When the soul doth meditate, it doth put forth*
*the rational acts; and then is the soul most like to God; for God*
*spends an eternity in contemplating His own essence*
*and attributes.*
*DR. BATES*

Suggested Hymns
*Be Still, My Soul*
*Jesus, Lover of My Soul*
*Spirit of God, Descend*

**1.** Biblical meditation is often conceived of as involving the whole life of the whole person. We saw that this was so in studies one and twenty-nine. Biblical meditation, however, is also presented in a narrower sense which focuses more on the inner life. Remembering that "mind," "heart," "spirit" and "soul" are all designations for the inner side, how is meditation especially related to the inner life in the following passages: Psalms 49:3; 77:6; 119:9-16; Colossians 3:15-17?

**2.** We have also developed various images of meditation in previous studies. How do the images of the tree, dwelling and feasting reflect this same concern of meditation with the inner person? Consider each of these images separately, recalling your previous meditations.

**3.** Because we see that meditation is so intimately involved with the inner life, we can learn much about meditation by studying references which develop the Bible's teaching on the inner man. For each of the following references, first locate the specific teaching about the inner life, then apply the insights to your understanding of meditation. The following questions could be a starting point.

☐ Ephesians 3:14-21. What effect does the Spirit have on the inner person (v. 16)? By what means does Christ dwell in our hearts (v. 17)? What effect does he have as he indwells us (vv. 17-19)? How are these effects similar to those of meditation?

☐ Romans 8:9-11. What results from the Spirit of God dwelling in us? What might occur from the Word of God dwelling in us through meditation?

**Further Study**

**1.** Read Psalm 51:6-12. What are the desires of the psalmist? Compare them with the desires of the psalmist in 119:9-16, 97-99.

**2.** Reflect on the following Proverbs which speak about the heart: 4:23; 15:13, 30; 16:21; 21:2.

**3.** Read Matthew 15:1-20 (esp. 17-19) and 23:25-28. What kinds of things do you suppose the Pharisees meditated on? How did they miss the point with regard to the inner life? Why?

# 31
# The Inner Life
## (Part II)

*Bless the LORD, O my soul; and all that is within me, bless*
*his holy name! Bless the LORD, O my soul, and forget not all*
*his benefits.*
PSALM 103:1-2

*For Paul the inward man means the soul and whatever*
*belongs to the spiritual life of the soul; just as the outward is*
*the body, with everything that belongs to it, health,*
*honours, riches, vigour, beauty, and such like.*
JOHN CALVIN

Suggested Hymns
*Blessed Be the Tie That Binds*
*I've Found a Friend*
*What a Friend We Have in Jesus*

**1.** In the final question of the previous study, we looked at several passages of Scripture to gain a proper understanding of the inner life essential to meditation. Now consider the following references with regard to both the inner life and meditation.

☐ 2 Corinthians 4:16—5:10. Recall study twenty-three on "dressing." Are there any insights from that study that might apply to this passage? Are you preparing to appear before Christ (5:10) by renewing the inner person through meditation?

☐ Matthew 12:33-37. How can meditation affect the fruit you produce? Recall your thoughts from studies twenty-one and twenty-seven on "tree" and "treasuring."

☐ Hebrews 4:12. As you meditate on the Word of God, what results should you expect in your life?

☐ Hebrews 10:15-17. How is the Word of God related to the inner life? What does this imply for meditation?

**2.** Perhaps you have noticed that many of these references to the inner life are dependent on and related to the redemptive work of Christ. If not, reconsider some of the references in question 1. Based on this observation, what must be one of the unique features of Christian meditation?

**3.** Read Galatians 4:6-7. Here are uniqueness of the Christian inner life is reflected on in terms of the intimate relationship with God which results from believing in Jesus. How does your inner life, and especially your meditation, reflect the intimacy of this relation to "Abba," the daddy or papa who is your heavenly Father?

**4.** How do dwelling and feasting amplify the intimacy involved in the Christian's inner life? Conclude by reading Revelation 3:20, where these two images are combined.

**Further Study**

**1.** Read Jeremiah 17:9, Romans 1:21 and Ephesians 4:17-19. What is the condition of the mind/heart of the unrepentant person? How does Psalm 119:130 offer hope to this situation?

**2.** What is especially important about the inner person in Romans 10:10? How is this idea further developed in Acts 16:14?

**3.** What characteristics or functions of the inner person are reflected in Proverbs 20:27, 1 Corinthians 2:11 and Psalm 64:6? What implications are there for meditation?

# 32
# Consistency

*At night his song is with me.*
*PSALM 42:8*

*Accustom yourself to a serious meditation every morning.*
*A fresh airing of our souls in heaven will engender in us*
*a purer spirit and nobler thoughts. A morning session will*
*serve us all day.... The thoughts of God were the*
*first visitors David had in the morning. God and his heart met*
*together as soon as he was awake and kept company*
*all the day after.*
*STEPHEN CHARNOOK*

Suggested Hymns
*Come, My Soul, Thou Must Be Waking*
*I Need Thee Every Hour*
*When Morning Gilds the Skies*

**1.** The principle of consistency has to do with when and how often we are to meditate. What do the following passages say about this principle: Psalms 1; 77:1-10; 119:97-99, 147-148; 145:1-7; Joshua 1:8? Notice also the occasions of these meditations.

**2.** What does Proverbs 6:20-22 have to teach us about when and how often we meditate, especially on God's Word? See also Proverbs 3:21-24, noting the time span and anticipated benefits of meditating on the wisdom found in Scripture.

**3.** Think about the image of feasting (study twenty-two), that is, eating and drinking. What does this image imply about the frequency or regularity of meditation? How does the image of investiture (study twenty-three), that is, putting off and on clothes, relate to the question?

**4.** Read John 15:1-11. What does the image of dwelling or abiding imply about consistency as a principle of meditation?

**Further Study**
**1.** What does Deuteronomy 6:1-9 teach us about the principle of consistency with regard to the Scriptures, specifically the law? Compare these verses with Proverbs 6:20-22. What similarities do you find?

# 33
# Prayer and Meditation
## (Part I)

*Let the words of my mouth and the meditation of my heart*
*be acceptable in thy sight,*
*O LORD, my rock and my redeemer.*
PSALM 19:14

*So anything that is to be done well ought to occupy the whole*
*man with all his faculties and members. As the saying*
*goes: he who thinks of many things thinks of nothing and*
*accomplishes no good. How much more must prayer*
*possess the heart exclusively and completely if it is to be a*
*good prayer!*
*MARTIN LUTHER*

Suggested Hymns
*Love Divine, All Loves Excelling*
*Take Time to Be Holy*

**1.** Prayer and meditation are interrelated in several ways. Wherever there is evidence of communion or communication with God, an occurrence of prayer will be assumed. There are, remember, various types of prayer: praise, thanksgiving, adoration, supplication, confession, commitment and so on. Many of the questions which follow may be quite difficult. In some cases you may need to meditate intensively on the psalms to answer them. Time and effort are part of the commitment we are called to in biblical meditation.
**2.** Psalm 145 was considered in study nineteen as a meditation on the works and glory of God (cf. esp. v. 5). Reread verses 1-7 and take note of the various forms of communion with God. What does the psalmist promise God he will do? Does he actually do what he promises? Look for evidence

of this in these initial verses and elsewhere throughout the psalm, making note of how the psalmist does in fact relate to God. Are there any promises that you should make to God?
**3.** Psalms 104 and 105 meditate on the works of God—Psalm 104 on the works of creation and providence, and Psalm 105 on the work of redemption. With the question of the relation between prayer and meditation in mind, meditate on these psalms. Pay special attention to the introductions, 104:1-4 and 105:1-7, and the conclusions, 104:31-35 and 105:45. What evidence of prayer do you see in these sections?
**4.** Summarize the findings on the relation of prayer to biblical meditation which you have discovered in this study. What other relationships have occurred to you from other studies?

**Further Study**
**1.** Psalms 77 and 143 were written in times of distress. Here, too, the interrelation of prayer and meditation is evident. Where in these psalms are the two spoken of and/or actually performed? Is it possible to distinguish where the one activity ends and the other begins? Explain. What criteria might you use as a basis for drawing such a distinction? Try to explain the connections between prayer and meditation which these psalms display.

# 34
# Prayer and Meditation
## (Part II)

*Make me understand the way of thy precepts,*
*and I will meditate on thy wondrous works.*
PSALM 119:27

*Meditation before prayer matures our conceptions, and*
*quickens our desires. Our heart is like a watch that is*
*soon run down, and needs constant winding up. It is an instru-*
*ment which is easily put out of tune. And meditation*
*is like the tuning of an instrument, and setting it for the*
*harmony of prayer. What is the reason that in prayer there is*
*such a slight discurrency in our thoughts, that our thoughts*
*are like dust in the wind, carried to and fro; but only*
*for want of meditation? What is the reason that our desires,*
*like an arrow shot by a weak bow, do not reach the mark?*
*But only this, we do not meditate before prayer; he that*
*would consider before he comes to pray, the things that he is*
*to pray for, pardon of sin, and the life of glory, how*
*would this cause his prayers to ascend like incense towards*
*God? The great reason why our prayers are ineffectual,*
*is because we do not meditate before them. David expresseth*
*prayer by meditation: "Give ear to my words, O Lord,*
*consider my meditation."*
*SALTER*

Suggested Hymns
*Open My Eyes That I May See*
*Sweet Hour of Prayer*

---

**1.** Often in the midst of meditation, the psalmist turns to address God in intimate, personal language. Notice the terms of address used in the following psalms of meditation: 119, 143, 145. Especially note the abundant use of personal pronouns—you, Thee, I, me, and so on. Look back over your previous study on the inner life (study thirty-one) for further examples. What do you think is the relationship among intimacy, prayer and meditation? In light of an unsearchable and majestic God (Ps 145), how can we be both respectful and intimate in *how* we pray and in *what* we pray?

**2.** What specific emphasis is added by the New Testament with regard to our relationship to God? Consider Romans 8: 14-17. How does this passage develop the idea of intimacy? What differences does the gift of the Spirit make for your prayer life (see Rom 8:26-27)? Are there implications for meditation?

**3.** Continue your consideration of Psalm 119. What does the psalmist specifically ask God for? Considering only the first four sections (vv. 1-32), make a list of the specific requests addressed to God. Be sure to look at verses 10, 12, 18, 22, 25-28. After you have compiled a list, try to classify these requests into types—for example, requests for teaching, understanding and so on. Consider your own prayer life. How does it reflect this variety?

**Further Study**

**1.** Consider the prayers of Paul and of Jesus in Ephesians 1:15-23, 3:14-20 and John 17:1-25. What evidence do you find for an intimate relation to God? for meditation? For instance, just where does the prayer of Ephesians 1 end?

**2.** Do you ever feel like your meditations are just not yielding fruit? You try, but you don't seem to get anything out of them? What encouragement might the following examples regarding prayer hold for you if applied to your life of meditation? Consult Luke 18:1-8, 22:44 and Hebrews 5:7.

**3.** Throughout the New Testament there are many promises given with regard to prayer. How do the following promises apply to your life of meditation? Consider John 14:12-14; 15:7, 16; 16:23-27. Based on these promises James adds further counsel. How does the counsel given in James 4:2-10 reflect on your life of meditation?

# 35
# Prayer and Meditation
## (Part III)

*May my meditation be pleasing to him,*
*for I rejoice in the LORD.*
*PSALM 104:34*

*Let meditation and prayer administer to our good actions,*
*and like oil to a lamp, give our charity fresh spirits and flame.*
*DR. LUCAS*

Suggested Hymns
*More Love to Thee, O Christ*
*Thy Loving-kindness, Lord, Is Good and Free*

**1.** In addition to quiet times of contemplation when the psalmist/meditator is alone with God (for example, Ps 62—63 and probably 27:4-5), two variations in the style of meditation and prayer are worth noting.

First, sometimes the devout may be alone with God, but the time is neither quiet nor inactive. Consider the opening few verses of Psalms 77 and 143. What do both of these introductions to the psalmist's meditations have in common? How is the psalmist bodily involved in his meditation (cf. esp. 77:2-4; 143:5-6)?

Second, sometimes the devout may not even be alone while meditating. Psalm 105, for instance, was likely used in the communal temple worship of Israel. We have seen that it is a meditation on the historical works of God. How could your times of worship and prayer, whether in small groups or in Sunday worship, be times of meditation? How and how often do you meditate while others pray? before you pray? during sermons? Do you often slip into daydreaming? How could you work to prevent this?

2. So extensive is the relation between prayer and meditation, that prayer can be seen as occurring before, during and after meditation. In the question above we saw that the meditations of Psalms 77 and 143 were begun with prayer. Throughout Psalm 119, which is a meditation on God's law from start to finish, you have found many evidences of prayer as an integral and natural part of the meditations. Now consider Psalms 19:14 and 104:34. These psalms close with prayers which refer to meditation. What is the concern of the psalmist in these closing prayers?

3. What implications do you draw for your own life from these prayerful meditations? Sit back now and reflect, meditate and pray about your life of meditation and prayer.

**Further Study**

1. The situations of Psalms 77 and 143 are quite similar. Look for further evidence for meditation which is "neither quiet nor inactive" in situations other than those of distress. Psalms 1 and 119 are good places to start.

# 36
# Song

Suggested Hymns
*Holy, Holy, Holy*
*I Sing the Mighty Power of God*
*O for a Thousand Tongues to Sing*

**1.** It is a very common experience among Christians to "sing psalms and hymns and spiritual songs" as part of worship. Such singing is also closely related to meditation, as will be seen from many of the passages already examined.

Psalms 104 and 105 were previously considered as meditations on the works of God. Notice how closely singing is related to meditation in verses 33-34 of Psalm 104, and verses 1-5 of Psalm 105. Psalm 104 is a more private meditation, while Psalm 105 was likely used in communal worship. Do your private meditations involve singing? If not, how might they? Do you meditate on the songs which are sung in group worship?

**2.** Colossians 3:16 speaks of meditation in terms of the Word of Christ richly dwelling within us. How is singing involved with meditation in this verse? What characterizes the attitude of this singing? To whom is the singing addressed in this verse? (Eph 5:18-21 is a parallel passage. Look at these verses for further insight.)

**3.** We have often seen in times of distress that the sufferer remembers and meditates on the faithfulness of God in the past. During these times, song is often present. How is song a part of meditation in Psalm 77, especially verse 6? Now look at Psalm 42 where the psalmist struggles with depression. Read through this psalm—notice the confident affirmation in verse 8. There the song is a prayer. How have you experienced a song in the night which is a prayer to God? Are there any songs which you consider "my song"? Why are these songs so special to you?

**4.** Psalm 119, which often has been our special example of meditation, also shows a special place of song. What does it say on this topic? Throughout the psalm the law of God is the object of meditation for the psalmist. What do God's "statutes" and "word" become in verses 54 and 172? When does this happen to your meditations? How do your desires and longings need to be more like the psalmist's?

**5.** Jonathan Edwards has said that "the duty of singing praises to God seems to be appointed wholly to excite and express religious affections. No other reason can be assigned why we should express ourselves to God in verse rather than in prose, and do it with music, but only that such is our nature and frame that these things have a tendency to move our affections." Do you agree? Why or why not? Consider testing this statement of Edwards by making singing a part of your daily devotions, if you haven't already. Spend some time flipping through a hymnal, reading the hymns at first and reflecting on their messages before singing. There is no need to feel restricted to special times for singing. Make those slack moments—washing dishes, driving to work, taking a study break—times of singing praise and drawing near to God. Remember that the psalmist in Psalm 1 delighted in

God's law, and so meditated on it day and night.

**Further Study**
**1.** Often special times of remembrance and celebration have issued in song for the people of God. Consider the role of song and meditation in such passages as Exodus 15 and Judges 5.
**2.** In what other passages does song play a particularly significant role in the worship and/or meditations of the people of God? Consider the role of song in the book of Revelation. Chapters 4 and 5 are a good place to start.

# 37
# Music and Other Sounds

*My mouth shall speak wisdom;*
*the meditation of my heart shall be understanding.*
*I will incline my ear to a proverb;*
*I will solve my riddle to the music of the lyre.*
PSALM 49:3-4

*Meditation is the tongue of the soul, and the language*
*of the spirit.*
*BISHOP TAYLOR*

Suggested Hymns
*The Heav'ns Declare Thy Glory*
*The Spacious Firmament on High*

**1.** As we noted in study five on Psalm 49, music and song often accompany meditation, and can be quite useful in solving some of the perplexities which confront us. Look back to that study to remind yourself of what you learned there.

**2.** Elsewhere in the Scriptures we find the benefits of music being employed. In 1 Samuel 16:14-23, David is called to play the harp for Saul. Why was David called by Saul? What was the effect of David's playing (v. 23)?

In 2 Kings 3:15 the prophet Elisha also uses music. Why did he call for a minstrel? What benefits did he anticipate from the music?

We, of course, are neither prophets like Elisha, nor are we usually terrorized by "an evil spirit from the Lord" as was Saul. But we may sometimes be afraid or weary like Saul, or want to seek God about a particular question as Elisha did. In such times we too may enjoy the benefits of music in our lives. How might music be helpful in your life now?

**3.** Music and song minister to our souls in ways which are often difficult to understand. Music can reach into our inner thoughts and affections and speak to us. Surely something is communicated to us, but it is not always easy to articulate the message. With Saul, a sense of refreshment, well-being and peace were communicated; for Elisha it was a state of mind receptive to the Spirit and Word of God.

According to Psalm 19, God's creation communicates in a similar way. Because nature is often an object of meditation (as we saw in studies nine through twelve), it would be especially helpful to examine this psalm more closely. Read Psalm 19 again, especially verses 1-6. What do the heavens communicate to David (v. 1)? How do they communicate? Have you meditated on the heavens and experienced this "music of the spheres"? Sunrise, sunset and clear night skies are especially good times for such meditations (cf. Ps 19:6; 8:3).

**4.** The sounds of nature are also often used in Scripture as descriptive of God's voice and presence. How is this so in Psalm 29? Read the description of the giving of the Law (which itself is so often an object of meditation; study eighteen) in Hebrews 12:18-21. This was indeed a frightening sight (v. 21) as the power and majesty of God were displayed. What have been your experiences of storms? What other sounds of nature display the "eternal power and deity" (Rom 1:20) of the Creator? As you meditate on creation in the future, remember to be aware of its sounds.

**Further Study**
**1.** Consider the usages of the sounds of nature in the following passages of Scripture: Psalm 93; Jeremiah 25:30-38; Isaiah 31:4.
**2.** Other Old Testament accounts of the giving of the Law are found in Exodus 19:16ff.; Deuteronomy 4:10-11; 5:2-5. Are these the same sounds as described in Hebrews 12? Do they have the same significance? Explain.

# 38
# Silence

*The* LORD *is in his holy temple;*
*let all the earth keep silence before him.*
HABAKKUK 2:20

*If the Holy Spirit should come when these thoughts are in your*
*mind and begin to preach to your heart, giving you* rich
and enlightened *thoughts, then give Him the honor, let your*
*preconceived ideas go, be quiet and listen to Him who*
*can talk better than you; and note what He proclaims and*
write it down, *so will you experience miracles as David says:*
*"Open my eyes that I may behold wondrous things out*
*of thy law" (Ps 119:18).*
*MARTIN LUTHER*

Suggested Hymns
*Be Still, My Soul*
*Let All Mortal Flesh Keep Silence*

**1.** In the last few studies we have looked at how prayer and meditation are related to song, music and other sounds. But how is silence—so often associated with our usual conceptions of meditation—involved? Perhaps you have gained some insight from the previous studies. Pause now to collect your thoughts on this topic.

**2.** Review Psalm 77. Often circumstances "force" the meditator to be silent. In verse 4 the psalmist "cannot speak."

In verse 3, was his soul quiet? at peace? resting? How essential is this silence to his meditation?

Look at the other two usages of *meditation* (vv. 6, 12). Do you notice any progression in the emotional tone of the psalm or in the silence of the psalmist?

**3.** In study four on Proverbs 1—9 we looked at the father's instruction to his son about wisdom. Throughout the passage the father calls on his son to hear his words of instruction. What implications concerning the role of silence in meditation can you draw from the following verses: Proverbs 1:8; 2:1-2; 4:1-2, 10, 20-21? What other expressions are parallel to *hear*? How is the silence implied in these verses more than simply keeping quiet?

4. Now read and meditate on Habakkuk 2:20. What attitude and activity are implied by the silence commanded? (Heb 12:28-29, Ps 27:4 and 63:2-4 may provide help on this question.) What does this verse imply about silence and your daily meditations? your corporate worship?

5. Summarize the teaching of this study and your own thoughts on silence in meditation. Perhaps a distinction between internal silence (in soul) and external silence (involving the body, especially the mouth) would be helpful.

**Further Study**

1. Continue your investigation of Proverbs 1—9 begun in question 3 above. Note especially Proverbs 2:3; 5:1, 7; 7:24; 8:4-7.

2. Rest is a topic commonly associated with silence. Consider the following passages for insight into the relation of silence to meditation: Matthew 11:28-30; Hebrews 3—4; Psalm 95.

3. Though the word *meditate* is not used in Psalm 62, what does the silence of verses 1 and 5 have to do with meditation? A review of "waiting" as discussed in study twenty-six may be helpful.

4. The book of Revelation pictures the fulfillment of all God's promises. The main chapters which present heavenly worship are 4—5, 19, 21—22. What are the appropriate responses presented in these passages? How is silence (or the lack of it) involved? How are your goals for meditation affected by this view of the "end product"?

# 39
# The Structure
# of Meditation

*I will call to mind the deeds of the LORD;*
*yea, I will remember thy wonders of old.*
*I will meditate on all thy work,*
*and muse on thy mighty deeds.*
PSALM 77:11-12

*A garment that is double dyed, dipped again and again,*
*will retain the colour a great while; so a truth which is the*
*subject of meditation.*
*PHILIP HENRY*

Suggested Hymns
*Blessing and Honor and Glory and Power*
*I Love to Tell the Story*
*Sing Them over Again to Me*

**1.** Studies two and three introduced the idea of meditation as a process. We looked at Psalm 119, noticing that there was much repetition in this psalm. Each moment of repetition, though, included an advance or at least a slight variation in the form of expression, and with that a new insight, perspective or application. This structure of repetition with variation is certainly fundamental in Psalm 119. Because of its many references to meditation (eight direct uses of the word), its object (the law) and its style (repetition and reflection), it is taken as the biblical example of meditation par excellence. In this study we will look at other psalms to see how repetition with variation is fundamental to biblical meditation.
**2.** In our earlier studies we introduced the often-used form of Hebrew poetry called *parallelism.* This is a special form of

repetition with variation. Look again at Psalm 77 (esp. vv. 1-12) noticing how repetition with variation is used. Try to write a definition of meditation using the insights you have gained from this psalm.

**3.** When we look at various psalms which clearly refer to meditation, we see a pattern similar to Psalm 119. Read Psalm 77 again. Three times the word for "meditate" occurs—verses 3, 6 and 12. (The Hebrew word which is translated "meditate" in verses 6 and 12 is sometimes rendered "sigh," as in verse 3.) In each of the three cases "meditate" is preceded by "I remember"—verses 3, 5 and 11. The psalmist seems to proceed with his meditation in stages—remembering and meditating, remembering and meditating, remembering and meditating. With each stage there is repetition and progress, until comfort is found. In what other ways do you see this progress? Consider the degree and type of articulation, the focus of attention and the degree of comfort found.

**4.** Not only is meditation a process of internal reflection and repetition, but the body also reflects or repeats the soul in its states and activities. How is this so in Psalm 63:1-8 and 143:5-6? How does the body reflect the soul in Psalm 1 and Psalm 119:15, 48, 97-104? In these latter verses (Ps 1 and 119) remember parallelism as you look for repetition. Such meditation takes time but has many rewards, as these verses make clear.

**5.** Have you noticed this pattern of repetition with variation in your own meditations? How might your awareness of this pattern affect your future meditating?

**Further Study**

**1.** Comment on St. Augustine's comment on Psalm 77. Speaking of meditation as "babbling," he says, "He babbled without, when he fainted; he babbled in his spirit within, when he advanced; he babbled on the works of God, when he arrived at the place toward which he advanced."

**2.** Review question 3 above. It may appear that the psalm ends rather abruptly. Does the ending (vv. 19-20) seem abrupt to you? How, if at all, does this ending resolve the trouble of the first verses? How might this be so?

Psalm 105, which is a meditation on the same theme as Psalm 77:11-20, ends in a different way, which may give a clue to our understanding of Psalm 77. To compare these two endings involves the work of meditation. Such meditation may or may not yield immediate fruit; but we have found this comparison a helpful exercise.

3. How is repetition with variation a significant feature of Psalm 1? Psalm 104? Psalm 105? Psalm 145?

4. Consider how Joshua's meditations were repeated by his bodily activities. (Note the command/obedience sequences throughout the book of Joshua.)

# 40
# Remembering

*I remember the days of old,*
*I meditate on all that thou hast done;*
*I muse on what thy hands have wrought.*
PSALM 143:5

*Meditating is that "remembering" so vital to praise.*
EDMUND P. CLOWNEY

Suggested Hymns
*The God of Abraham Praise*
*Here, O My Lord, I See Thee Face to Face*
*O Day of Rest and Gladness*

**1.** Throughout three psalms which we have previously considered (Ps 63:6; 77:3, 6, 12; 143:5) we find *remember* parallel to *meditate*. (Remember that *remember* may be translated "think of" in some versions [e.g. RSV, Jerusalem Bible, New English Bible], but none of these do so consistently.) Based on what you have learned about parallelism how would you say *remember* and *meditate* are related in these psalms? What similarities and differences do you find in each line of the parallels? Would you say that the versions which read "think of" (or a similar expression) are justified in such a rendering when the basic meaning of the word is simply "remember"?
**2.** Where in Psalm 119:9-16 do you find reference to the involvement of the memory? How does this expression contribute to your idea of memorization? How does this view of

remembering relate to the question of verse 9? to the meditating of verse 15? to the not forgetting of verse 16? How do the
parallelisms throughout this section further enrich your
understanding of remembering in its relation to meditation?
**3.** The New Testament celebration of the Lord's Supper is a
feast of remembrance. This is especially clear in Paul's account in 1 Corinthians 11:23-26. How so? What is the full content of this remembrance? In what ways is this remembrance
similar to meditation? Review for instance studies fifteen,
twenty and twenty-two. Has the celebration of this sacra-
ment been a significant experience for you? How could your
new understanding of remembrance and meditation contribute to your Christian life in this regard?
**4.** Remembrance also plays a significant part in the Ten
Commandments. Read Exodus 20:1-17. How is this so in the
prologue of verse 1? How is this so in verses 8-11? For further insight into the meaning of *remember*, compare the account of this fourth commandment found in Deuteronomy
5:12-15. How does this comparison correlate with what we
have found with regard to meditation? (Reflect back on
studies twenty-four and twenty-five.)

In the New Testament, the Lord's Day (our Sunday) re-
places the sabbath of the Old Testament. How have the objects of special remembrance found in Exodus 20 and Deuteronomy 5 been changed by the person and work of Jesus?

John Calvin states that one purpose of the Lord's Day is
"that every individual, as he has opportunity, may diligently
exercise himself in private, in pious meditation on the works
of God." Do you find this conclusion in keeping with the Old
Testament command to "remember"? If so, how might you
use Sunday more fully as a special time of meditation?
**5.**   You are now at the end of these meditations on meditation. Pause to remember and reflect on what you have
learned. Are there points which you need to make special
note of now? Are there points which you have already for-
gotten? Reviewing your notebook or journal can itself be an

occasion for rich meditation and thanksgiving to God.

**Further Study**
**1.** Consider the following quote from Thomas Watson. "The Sabbath-day is for our interest; it promotes holiness in us. The business of week-days makes us forgetful of God and our souls: the Sabbath brings him back to our remembrance. When the falling dust of the world has clogged the wheels of our affections, that they can scarce move towards God, the Sabbath comes, and oils the wheels of our affections, and they move swiftly on. . . . The Sabbath is a friend to religion; it files off the rust of our graces; it is a spiritual jubilee, where-in the soul is set to converse with its Maker." How true is this of your own experience? Consider Isaiah 58, especially verses 13-14, for further insight on the sabbath.
**2.** This same Watson, in his discussion of the uses of the sab-bath, defines meditation as "the soul's retiring within itself, that, by a serious and solemn thinking upon God, the heart may be raised up to divine affections." In light of your stud-ies of meditation, how good a definition do you think this is? Try to write such a definition in your own words.
**3.** How are Psalms 25, 34 and 37 meditations? Taking these psalms one at a time, what elements of meditation do you find in them?